EVERYBODY NEEDS A COACH

OVERCOMING THE ODDS IN YOUR LIFE

KENNETH G. BORDEAUX

ARPress
ILLUMINATING IDEAS
EMPOWERING VOICES

ARPress
45 Dan Road Suite 5
Canton MA 02021
Hotline: 1(888) 821-0229
Fax: 1(508) 545-7580

Ordering Information:

Quantity sales. Special discounts are available on quantity purchases by corporations, associations, and others. For details, contact the publisher at the address above.

Printed in the United States of America.

ISBN-13:   Softcover   979-8-89330-298-1
             eBook   979-8-89330-297-4
Library of Congress Control Number: 2024901592

EVERYBODY NEEDS A COACH

OVERCOMING THE ODDS IN YOUR LIFE

TABLE OF CONTENTS

ACKNOWLEDGMENTS

First, I would like to acknowledge all the "Coaches" that have played a part in my life. When I thought about this list, I realized that I had so many coaches. For the sake of space and time, I have narrowed down my list to just a few. If you are an everyday person like me with good qualities and flaws, you would probably be the first to understand why I have had to have so many people who have coached me in one way or another.

Always, I have to thank my cousin, editor and publisher–Judith Smith who has coached me into writing several books. Judith, I feel like we are getting closer by the day as we have worked together in the past few years of my life. You have always been there since we met in 2004. It is your coaching and guidance that has gotten me this far in expressing myself on paper. I really cannot believe we are publishing our third book together in such a short time. Thank you for your continued hard work and dedication. *"You are a great book writing Coach!"*

To my uncle, Bishop Dennis C. Bordeaux; since I was a boy, you have coached me as a son and not a nephew. I've learned so much from you. Thank you for the times you had the wisdom to intervene in my life. Thank you so much for being *prophetic and not pathetic*. I have not forgotten when you said to me, *"Pull back the reigns!"* I have never ridden in a horse and buggy; but I had sense enough to know that pulling back the reigns had to do with stopping or slowing down. I want you to know that I heard you. Stopping and slowing things down is now a part of my life. Thanks for your boldness. *"You are a great Uncle, Pastor-Coach!"*

To my late mother, Carol F. Bordeaux; you have been more than just a mom. You have been a confidant and a big sister. I feel like we all grew up together. Maybe that's why the bond between us was sometimes toxic and strong. You've coached me on life, responsibility, love and relationships. I want you to know that I learned a lot from you. You have been there for all of your children. We know that you want the best for all of us. Thank you for your strong support, words of wisdom and direct counsel. I am so glad that your body received my kidney as if it was your own and you got another three years on life. Rest in peace! "*You have beena great Mother, Sister and Life-Coach!*"

To my oldest brother, Jeffery B. Bordeaux; I know you might be shocked. But when I was thinking about this list, I could not help think about the few words of counsel you gave me when I was going through with my own family. What I could not hear from you when I was younger, trust me, I sure hear it now. Maybe it's because you changed the way you give advice or I changed the way I listen to you. I know you love me and want the best for me. I want you to know that I heard you when you told me in your own way "to not be a sucker." I want you to know that this time around I got it. Thank you for your support in the time of chaos. "*You have been a much needed Big Brother Coach!*"

To my baby sister Nicole J. Bordeaux; I am proud of you and also how you have bounced back and *handled your business*. You have accomplished a lot, just from a little advice that I gave to you after you graduated from high school. You have made great strides and continue to do so. I have watched you as well and I want to thank you for showing me how to pull back order and structure in your life despite the setbacks. "*You are a great big-little sister coach by example!*"

To my oldest sister in Nashville, Brenda Beene; Brenda I am just going to come out and say, "You are so wise." I wish I had grown up with you. Half of the mistakes I made in relationships would not have happened if I had been around you. But we all have to live and learn. You see things that others do and know things that many do not know. You have no idea what it did for me when you simply said to me what you heard in your heart, "*All things work for the good of those who love God and are called according to his purpose.*" Sis, you were so right. I knew it was not just your voice, but the voice of God speaking through you to me. Thanks for being a prophetic sister and coach. Your husband, Beene is a blessed man and I have witnessed how much he loves my sister. He's not going anywhere; he knows that he got it right this time. *"You are a great Big Sister-Coach!"*

To James Clark; we fuss, we debate, but at the end of the day you are still the oldest and the big brother God gave in Colorado. You keep me sharp and remind me of things like no other. You really do make me think and evaluate all things from a broader perspective. I appreciate your simple approach to life; it keeps me balanced and out of the doctor's office. We both know, I can tend to go a little off on the deep end sometimes, but you keep me from going too far. Thanks for being a voice of wisdom, coach and friend. I salute you too for your role in my life that established the necessity of this book. *"You are a great Big Brother away from home Coach!"*

To my best of friend, roommate in the Air Force and adopted brother—Kwaku. God gave you watch over me at 18. Thank you for supporting me and inspiring me with my dreams to get a college education. You jumped right in and assisted me with my studies from day one. I want you to know that meant a lot to me to meet someone that supported me and not laughed at me because I had a dream to be educated. I have learned from your study habits and work ethic. I saw early on from your accomplishments that you had to work hard first and have fun later. I know that your two boys, Andrew, now in the Air Force Academy, and Johnathan, who has shown that he can be accepted in any Ivy League school in America, are making you proud. You have also been there in the tough times with counsel. I am truly blessed to have you as a best of friend and confidant. *You are a great big brother, no nonsense, Get-Your–Act-Together Coach.*

To my Cousin Beverly; you have been a great inspiration, lately, in my life. You have a load of wisdom that I enjoy listening to. I want you to know that I keep everything that you have taught me in mind. It's a blessing to hear things from an older woman's perspective. Know that you have coached me well. Because of you, I am better prepared for love and relationships. Thank you. *"You are a great Cousin Coach!"*

To Dr. Tim Bagwell; we have known each other for a long time. Little did we know when we first met in 1997 that we both enjoyed watching and coaching football. I might have won more games than you though. How about 85% from age 5 to 12 for starters? That's pretty tough to beat. Anyway, I know you had to be tough on those boys to make the playoffs and championship each year. I just cannot imagine you coaching and accepting anything less than that. It just does not fit your personality. You might want to call and check up on each child and make sure that none of them are permanently damaged because they had to meet your *"no less than Super Bowl"* expectations (LOL). I see that your son Adam is following in your footsteps with his son. I want you to know that I have had some incredible times with you as a spiritual son at *Word of Life*. You have coached me through my highs and lows, through the times of light and days of pitch black darkness. I really do believe that your coaching, pushing and prodding over the years is a big reason why this gift of writing for kingdom of God business has manifested in my life. I never knew it was there and ready to come out until you pushed it out of me through your preaching and teaching. You never change. You're always the same. You refuse to allow your sheep to settle, but push us into higher heights and new experiences for the Lord's workings. I am truly a beneficiary of your anointed service and will always be grateful to have you and Gayla as kingdom leaders. Keep pushing and prodding us like you always have and do not let us settle. *"You are one of the greatest Pastor, Teacher Coaches alive!"*

To one of my latest coaches that God has put in my life, Dr. Frank Summerfield, *Word of God Christian Church, Raleigh, NC.* All I can say to you my brother is …*Wow!* You put words and scriptures to many things I had been pondering over for years. How you articulate what was only a figment of my imagination is incredible. You are really a great teacher, pastor and most of all you are a *"Coach for the up and coming kings in the Kingdom."* How you do all this and remain so cool? God is the only answer. You are just getting started. The world is going to know you and your kingdom spouse. I salute you both. There is still a whole lot left to do. Get ready! *You too are a great Pastor, Teacher Coach.*

To my writing, grammar and speech coach, Rosalind. It would be neglectful if I did not write to you about the grammatical and verbal coaching skills you have given me for the past few years. You are one of the brightest, most serious, and funniest women I know. You came in and cleaned up a lot of my verbal and grammatical errors, not to be critical of me, but to make my life and work better. Notre Dame, Cornell, the University of Rochester and Toastmasters have taught you well. I know that I am not where you would like me to be with my speech and grammar yet, but I feel that it is going in the right direction. *You are a great writing, teacher and friend Coach.*

Finally, to my lifelong coach, Mr. Robert Brown; you did not know this, but it was you who inspired me to write this book in the first place. It was in your living room that night while watching Monday Night Football that I got the revelation to write this book. It was that then that I realized how selflessly you have been a coach to me and others who would listen for many years. I cannot tell you how much I have enjoyed your willingness to impart your thoughts in my life since I was about 15 years old. Whether it was on a street corner, in a restaurant, or in your own living room, you have been coaching men for years. I realize how blessed I am to have had someone like you as a mentor, father figure and coach to discuss life and its twist and turns. You have given me much advice down through the years. I want you to know that I am doing everything I can to carry out your advice. I appreciate the love, concern and fellowship we have had since I was a teenager. I want to give you your flowers while you are still living. Near or far, I will always cherish my time with you. Thank you, sir, for everything; you have been a great father coach and big part of my foundation and belief system when it comes to work and family. I wish that all young men and women had a great coach like you. You made me realize that night, *"Everybody Needs a Coach."*

INTRODUCTION

Writing is starting to become apart of my blood now that I have completed *Choose*, *Choose II* and *The Spirit of Greed*. As soon as I completed *The Spirit of Greed*, I began to outline my newest book: *Everybody Needs a Coach*. The first three books have more of a serious tone to them. I feel that this book will have a humorous side and also tackle some serious issues.

If you have read any of my other books, you know that I am a coach. I have coached young men for many years, eighteen years to be exact. My life has been guided by the basic principles of coaching since I was about 10 years old.

When I think about life, experience and expertise: none of it is perfected in us without someone else who has walked down that path teaching us. If we think about all that comprises man's experiences on earth, if we do not have a coach in just about every experience, we are left out here running against the wind.

There is no one person who has it all and does not need coaches, teachers, or leaders in their life.

Coaching is a unique ability that I believe God gives to those who have learned from certain life experience. I also think that coaching can be a tricky craft that can easily be coveted by those who are still in the learning phase of perfecting a specific area in their life. Let's be honest. The ability to teach something can be rather exciting and desirable by people who may not be ready for the task.

When I was a little boy, I was so impressed with my *Pop Warner Football Coach*, Mr. Paizano. He had a unique ability to pull the best out of each young boy on our team and make him want to play the game of football. Mr. Paizano taught me things like team work, responsibility and discipline. These are values that I would never forget and would later use in life to teach my own little league players twenty years later.

I do not want you to think that I am referring only to coaching sports. I found that everybody needs a coach in just about every area of their lives.

Some people will be a coach to you in one way and there will be others who will be a coach to you in other ways. The point is that we are always learning. We are always growing. The mind that accepts that it needs to be trained in this life will win.

All successful people that I have known all have one thing in common; they have several people in their lives that have more success than them. They are constantly looking to learn more. I have never met a successful man that has no wise confidant in his or her life. To be honest with you, if it had not been for the wise men and women that I experienced have in my life, I do not think I would be writing this book.

I have been very fortunate to meet and know some very intelligent people. I have also been just as unfortunate to meet quite the opposite. If I were to weigh the good with the bad I could easily choose to focus on the good. People that I have met, some are now deceased, took great valued interest in my life and it has helped me to be able to focus on appropriate things.

I am reminded by something that I read in the Bible when Martha was prodding Jesus to deal with her sister Mary about helping her with the preparations of the house.

> *As Jesus and his disciples were on their way, he came to a village where a woman named Martha opened her home to him. She had a sister called Mary, who sat at the Lord's feet listening to what he said. But Martha was distracted by all the preparations that had to be made. She came to him and asked, Lord, do not you care that my sister has left me to do the work by myself? Tell her to help me! Martha, Martha, the Lord answered, You are worried and upset about many things, but only one thing*

is needed. Mary has chosen what is better, and it will not be taken away from her.[1]

I like what Jesus said to Martha. This is the principle that will serve as the foundation of the entire book. If there is one thing I have been able to do because of Coach Paizano's gift and love for us as young boys. I have learned to recognize honest wisdom and from time to time, sit at its feet and choose to listen to it speak.

You would think it would be natural for people to recognize wisdom and want to invest their time in hearing what it has to say. I have recognized in my life that that is not so great a passion in a lot of people's lives.

I am writing *"Everybody Needs a Coach"* to point out the importance of a "life coach" and the different things that you need to know to overcome the odds in your life.

I have no idea who this may reach, but I am certain it will help somebody. Maybe you do not have a coach in your life. Some have never had a coach. You could have had good coaches around you with different expertise and maybe you did not utilize them. I do not know what your or someone else's situation maybe. What I do know is that I have been inspired to write this book. As basic as this may sound, we cannot assume that people understand that they need a coach.

We are living in a time when many are approaching this world defying any and every attempt of someone trying to teach them. Thank God, that certain people have helped me all throughout my life. I have always had an open ear to people who I realized had an honest interest in my life.

The world is still full of many good people. You do not have to lend your listening ear to those you know that truly do not have your best interest at hand. Good people are all around us. If you are doing what you are supposed to in life, you will have a solid hand full of people that truly have your best interest.

The relationships that you will gather will only add to a greatly formed nucleus of people that can coach you in many ways throughout your years. Join me in the next several chapters as I write to you things I have learned and why everybody needs a coach.

---

1   *Luke 10:38-41*

CHAPTER 1

A Coach for Correction
Correction is What Makes a Champion

"When Peter came to Antioch, I opposed him to his face, because he was clearly in the wrong."

~ Galatians 2:11

I am reminded of a very good book that I read a few years ago entitled: *"Be Quick, but Do not Hurry "*by Andrew Hill. The book is about coaching and life principles by the legendary UCLA Basketball Coach, John Wooden.

John Wooden has been one of the most beloved basketball coaching icons in college basketball history. One of the principles I noticed that Coach Wooden would demonstrate is how the team should run an offensive play, pass the ball, block out or defend.

He would demonstrate it to the players first; afterward, he would have the players repeatedly practice what he demonstrated over and over again. He would make corrections to what the players did. The interesting point this book makes is that he would then disappear and sit way up in the basketball arena where the players could not see him and watch them constantly do what he had just taught and demonstrated. He would then have a larger view of other things that needed to be corrected. Next, he would come back down out of the stands and make those corrections.

I too found this type of coaching useful and successful when coaching kids or adults in football. I could take a child as young as 5 years of age and a man as old as 35 years of age and show them the proper way to catch a football. I taught my own boys at an early age how to properly catch, throw, tackle and run passing routes.

It was fun to do and see them learn; however none of this comes without correction. You cannot be willing to teach someone what to do and not be willing to put in the work to correct them so they can do it right. Having a coach or coaches in your life is something that we all need so we can do things right.

When you think of a coach, they are people who know more about a subject than you. No coach can teach someone who feels they have more knowledge than them on the subject. We call these lost souls—"un-coachable."

Peter, in the story at Antioch, had been corrected by the Apostle Paul on a matter that could harm the development of the new church. The Apostle Peter had a way of acting one way in front of the Jewish Christians and another way with the Gentile believers. We called this being two-faced when I was a kid.

He would not embrace his Gentile brothers in the presence of the Jewish believers. Paul, having more understanding on the development of the church than Peter, saw his duplicity and corrected him. He knew how he was treating his Gentile Christian brothers in front of the Jews was clearly wrong. In fact, what Peter was doing had nothing to do with the truth of who all the gospel was intended for. Paul, though chosen after Peter, had more insight into Jewish law and customs. Therefore, once enlightened, Paul understood the revelation of the purpose of Christ to the Gentiles as well.

Paul gives his Jewish credentials in these words:

> *If anyone else thinks he has reasons to put confidence in the flesh, I have more: circumcised on the eighth day, of the people of Israel, of the tribe of Benjamin, a Hebrew of Hebrews; in regard to the law, a Pharisee; as for zeal, persecuting the church; as for legalistic righteousness, faultless.* [2]

2   *Philippians 3:4-6*

What Paul was trying to let the people of Philippi know is that he too erred in the faith under the Law of Moses and came to understand that salvation came through Christ as a free gift to all men, without the need for the works of the flesh.

Which brings me to this other point, coaches are people of integrity. Not only are they the people who are not afraid to mention their mistakes, but they are the people in your life that love you enough to confront you when you do wrong.

People who turn away and endorse you in your wrong doings are not doing you any favors at all. I believe that **correction is what makes a champion**. It takes experience to figure this out. Coaches are there to make sure that you are doing things right. They keep you or get you back on course.

Peter had clearly gotten off course with the truth of the gospel. He was embarrassed to embrace his Gentile brothers in front of his Jewish clique. It was not right or keeping in line with the destiny of the gospel. The gospel had come to both Jew and Gentiles. Peter was supposed to project that to not one group, but both, regardless of whose presence he was in.

It is amazing how when we get around one group we act one way and when we are around another group we conduct ourselves in another. Paul did not care. His heart and mind was focused on the truth of Jesus Christ. He did not waste time rebuking the Jews, but instead, turned to Peter and put him in his place.

Paul knew that it was Peter's leadership that was making the Jewish believers go astray. When there is a mess, sometimes you have to turn to the person who should know better and correct them. They may not like it, but they will be left to deal with the correction themselves.

Leaders are responsible for teaching others right and wrong. This is why the enemy loves to try to discredit leaders. He knows that they have a greater purpose. If he can discredit the leader, then the people will not listen to learn the truth. Leaders have to be resilient in their effort to keep standing on the Word of God. Allow God the time to sort out confusion himself.

Correction from a coach is a good thing. It is for discipline. Even God our Father believes in the fruit that comes from correction. Here is what the writer says in the book of Hebrews 12: 4-13:

In your struggle against sin, you have not yet resisted to the point of shedding your blood. And you have forgotten that word of encouragement that addresses you as sons:

My son, do not make light of the Lord's discipline, and do not lose heart when he rebukes you, because the Lord corrects those he loves, and he punishes everyone he accepts as a son.Endure hardship as a discipline; God is treating you as sons. For what son is not disciplined by his father? If you are not disciplined then you are illegitimate children and not true sons. Moreover, we have all had human fathers who disciplined us and we respected them for it. How much more should we submit to the Father of our spirits and live!

> *Our fathers disciplined us for a little while as they thought best; but God disciplines us for our good, that we may share in His holiness.*

> *No discipline seems pleasant at the time. Later on, however, it produces a harvest of righteousness and peace for those who have been trained by it*

> *Therefore, strengthen your feeble arms and weak knees. Make level paths for your feet, so that the lame may not be disabled, but rather healed.[3]*

During my years of playing Pop-Warner football, I learned discipline on the practice field. Our coaches did not teach us that it was ok to miss practice, games, or to be late. In fact, the entire time I played, I never was late to a practice, a game or dared to miss a practice or game day. I learned discipline. Was it hard at times? Yes, it was.

I've visited the corner I used to stand at as a kid waiting for the bus to come and take me to practice. I was there everyday with my uniform on and helmet in my hand. Little did I know that being a part of Pop-Warner was shaping my life into becoming a responsible adult.

I traveled to practice further than anybody on our team. I came from a different side of town than most of the kids on my team. All

---

3   *Hebrews 12:12-13*

the other kids lived near the practice field. I would be the first to get there and the last to get home every night, but I did it. I took the responsibility myself to get where I needed to be, including on game day. I started learning this at age 10. My coaches did not accept any excuses.

Unfortunately, we are living in a day and time where the kids are not appreciative of such training and correction is not readily received. I recognize that we live with a more sensitive generation than in the past. People's voices want to be heard, even if what they are saying is foolishness.

The idea of being corrected seems to cause more hurt than good. What has happened to us in this day and time? Correction does not necessarily have to mean anything physical, but it more importantly means you have someone in your life that pulls you back in line when you appear to be going off the good path. The people that do this are your coaches. You should be thankful to God for them.

No one is paid to keep us on the straight and narrow. Sometimes you just need good advice; and if you are going about something wrong, then the coaches you have around you can correct what you are thinking and doing.

Understand, true coaches will never leave you, that is, if you are worth of the stay. They are always there; they do not necessarily come looking for you either. Many times you have to go to them. It is up to us to establish the mentor—student relationship with them and work within those parameters. That is your responsibility, not theirs.

Sometimes roles change, but mostly, you should have people who are the coach and you are the student. Jesus taught this principle to the people: A student is not above his teacher, but everyone who is fully trained will be like his teacher.[4] The purpose of you having coaches in your life is so that you can be fully trained and become like or similar to your coach. The only way you become like your coaches is to pay attention to what they say.

In today's world, the attention of our young people is focused on those who have money, music, fame, but no character. I will not deal with that issue here. You have to read my book, *The Spirit of Greed*, to

---

4   *Luke 6:40*

get that information. Coaches look to duplicate their efforts and build character. They have spent considerable time in learning what works. That's why it's good to have more than one coach in your life. We need to pull disciplines from each one and use them for our success.

I would have to say that I am still very optimistic about God raising up more leaders who can influence the world to good and bring correction to the way we have conducted business and live our lives.

The bottom line is that if you have coaches in your life, then you are not above your coach. God is the one who put certain people in our lives to teach us and correct us when we are wrong. To all the good coaches out there, keep coaching and stay strong. Whether the world realizes it or not, it still needs you to make its champions.

CHAPTER 2

A Coach for Accountability

"In those days Israel had no king, everyone did as he saw fit."

~ Judges 17:6

I f you would read the book of Judges, chapters 17 through 21, you will see what happens to a people when there is no one in leadership in a nation. The Israelites, due to his death, had just lost Sampson as judge over Israel. They began to live in a time when there was no king, ruler, or authority over Israel. Because there was no king, ruler, or governance over the people, there was disorder in every evil way.

"Everyone did as he saw fit."[5] This was a mess. They had no political, social, religious, or household order. Everything that people did was at their own discretion. If they thought it was right they did it. Micah, the priest, had no priestly order. He went off and became the priest of a single man's household and worshipped idol gods. This was the nation's priest relinquishing his priestly duties for the nation to become a priest in a foreigner's home. Sex, violence, and crime in the nation were out of control. Micah and his concubine are welcomed to stay at an older gentlemen's home. The men of Gibeah came to the house demanding that the man send out the Levite priest so they can have sex with him.

These guys did not ask for the woman, instead they asked for the man, the priest. They were insistent on having sex with the priest. Instead, Micah sent out his concubine and they raped her and abused her throughout the night. The woman would die from the abuse and Micah would cut up her body and send parts to all 12 tribes of Israel. They were clearly out of control.

There was no regard for anybody during this time. Israel had no judge in place. They had no accountability and controls.

The point that I am making is where there is no law, there is no order. One of my favorite television shows is *"Law & Order: Special Victims Unit."* I love to watch this show when I have a chance. The show is about what goes on in the streets of New York City where they also shoot the film. Unfortunately, New York has a reputation of being a state where crime is prevalent due to an evil, harsh, and short-fused culture of people.

In defense of my fellow New Yorkers, I would say that New Yorkers by and large are very friendly people. You have to get to know them; however, they just do not trust people very easily. Coaches in your life bring law & order. More importantly, they bring accountability. Accountability can almost be a curse word for much of today's generation. There was a time when bringing young people into account for their actions as adults, leaders, teachers, neighbors and parents was just apart of the culture. Nowadays, things have changed. People do not seem to want to do that as adults anymore. Bringing a young person to account as an adult today could put you in a position where you're almost standing alone. Young people today go off and curse out their parents for bringing them into account for things they should be doing, but are not. Yet, these same parents, relatives and adults spend good money on these rebellious children; buying them cell phones, electronic tablets, tennis shoes, and new clothes. Unfortunately, these children are so lost in their bad behavior that you have to allow them to dig their own graves and allow life's hell teach them. You can only teach kids who want to be taught and coach children who want to be helped.

Accountability is something that was apart of my life. Thank God it was there for me. I did not realize just how much people defy it. We are living in a world where so many do not want to answer to anyone. What a crazy time we are living in! We have to understand that accountability will not hurt you. It will certainly not destroy who you are if you have people who you answer to. We find the desire to be unaccountable in our homes, marriages, workplace, business, churches, ministries, organizations, government and the like. To be accountable would be a good thing for us all. It gives you some measures, boundaries, and controls for when you are in the difficult seasons of your life. Many times when we are going through things, we cannot always depend on our own thoughts to come up with the best solutions.

When the storms are raging in your life, we are more apt to make a bad decision over a good one. Coaches in your life, who you are accountable to, can help you process through the storm.

Notice, I said coaches, not roaches! Coaches are the people in your life who have your best interest. Coaches do not have to be near, they can be far. They are the people you can call or go visit for a checkin. Roaches are the people in your life that can only make you filthy. They enjoy whatever filth they can get you into. They do not serve any real purpose but for destruction. Roaches are good at bringing in more filth. They come in groups. I know this is not the most desirable way to put this, but you get my point!

It is important to keep your life free of nasty roaches and lean towards your coaches. A true coach does not always tell you what you want to hear. They do not readily submit to your thoughts, feelings or emotions. A true coach is focused on what is right and best for you. People that appease your flesh are not coaches. The flesh is full of the mess and filth in our lives. Once again, roaches love mess. They are willing and ready to have a group session about things that are unfruitful and are very ungrateful. They feed off their past hurts and the pain. A coach is just the opposite. He or she will focus on how you can be delivered from the mess. A roach will never lead you to be a champion.

Let's look at this analysis in the form of ministry. I have coached and been in the ministry since 1991. I enjoy studying and teaching the word of God. For me it is a good fit. Since I did not attend church as a child or teenager, when I became a Christian at 20 years of age, I knew that I was far behind and began to study the Bible a lot. Out of that hunger and thirst for biblical knowledge evolved a ministry gift on my life. I am not ashamed of it; in fact, I am very proud of it. But along with this gift, I realize not everyone has had the privilege, opportunity, or know how, to study God's word, therefore, I teach it to those who have an ear to hear.

Make no mistake about it; there are spiritual advantages in knowing God's word. I have noticed in my somewhat significant tenure in ministry that a lot of clergy preach to appease the flesh, emotions, and feelings of the people. They do not teach them how to get out of their emotional downfall.

Unfortunately, the people are stroked in a way that keeps them in bondage. It is like clergy are afraid if the person is set free, they will no longer need their services.

True coaches, whether they are pastors, leaders, fathers, mothers, grand-parents, school teachers, friends, or business associates, always look at your expected end. They counsel you from the vantage point of getting you where you need to be and not keeping you where you are.

Successful coaches look at the big picture. Seasonal coaches do not. They look at the here and now, but not where you should be going. Bishop TD Jakes, although he appeals to the mental and emotional needs of the people, has a great gift of pushing you to the life you ought to live. He is very adept in the ministry of Christ and His purpose. Bishop Jakes never leaves you where you are, but he will challenge you to get to where you should be. My Pastor, Dr. Tim Bagwell, is another example I have had the privilege of knowing over the years of my ministry who does the same. Dr. Bagwell never licks your wounds or "kisses your boo-boo" as a believer, but constantly focuses on thrusting you into your prophetic purpose. My uncle, Bishop Dennis C. Bordeaux, has for years challenged his congregation to rise above their emotions and live in the Spirit.

The list goes on and on of a host of people I have had in my life to coach me. We should never have the leisure of throwing in the towel and giving up on life. It is a blessing to have those who push you forward despite your losses.

We do not realize how many people give up on life daily. They do not realize if they just hang in there for a little while longer, their greatest opportunity is just around the corner. My mother would always say "We can see down the street, but God can see around the corner."

We need coaches for accountability in our lives. Whether it's for personal, spiritual, vocational, marital, relational, or financial accountability, we need it.

When you have accountability to those who coach you, you will more thoughtfully consider all that you do and how you do it. I will not say that everything will always work out right. What I am saying is when trouble comes, you will be able to navigate your way through the messes of life well.

I have found that those who have no accountability do not care to thoughtfully consider what they do. These peple have no desire to answer to anyone. It is about what they feel and what they are able to do as they see fit. This is a spirit that brings lawlessness into our homes, churches, businesses, schools and communities.

You can never get anywhere without order. Even if you are taking a trip across the country, you must have order. It would be mindless to start in Missouri, then travel by way of Florida to get to California. That is what happens when we do not have accountability in our lives. We set out aimlessly fighting towards a target that we cannot seem to hit.

Let's not be like Israelites after the days of Sampson. They had no leader, no king, and everyone did what was right in his own eyes.

I would like to think that no accountability brings chaos. Where there is chaos there is disorder, confusion and every evil practice. God has not called us to disorder, but to order. He has not called us to confusion, but perfection.

When He led Israel out of Egypt, He knew exactly which direction they needed to go to get to the Red Sea. The Israelites would have never wandered in the desert for 40 years if they would have remained accountable to the Law of Moses. You can argue that point if you want, but I have read the Bible. The wandering in the desert came because they wanted to prove to Moses that they knew God too. In their eyes, Moses was no one to be telling them what to do; therefore, they focused in on his faults and justified their reasons to free themselves of the law that was binding unto them. Because of this rebellion, they ended up detaining themselves 40 years in the wilderness.

Live free and come alive! Humble yourself and submit yourself to people you are accountable to.

CHAPTER 3

A Coach is for Instruction

"Finally, brothers, we instructed you how to live in order to please God, as in fact you are living. Now we ask you and urge you in the Lord Jesus to do this more and more. For you know what instructions we gave you by the authority of the Lord Jesus."

~ 1 Thessalonians 4:1-2

For several days, I had been waiting in quietness and expectation on how and what the Lord would reveal for me to write in this chapter. I find it very interesting that if we wait for the Spirit's leading, He will reveal things to us that we have long forgotten.

One thing about my home town is that if you have not seen someone in many years, there are a few places that you can sort of hang out and there is no telling who you might see walk in. One of the places is a good take out dinner restaurant. I had just come from a Friday night Bible study and was sitting with one of my sisters in Christ eating *"Country Sweet"* chicken, when I heard a young man speak to a couple that had just walk in the door.

The young man said to the older couple who had walked inside of the restaurant, *"Hey, Mr. Nix."*

I thought to myself, *"Mr. Nix?"*

I turned and asked the older gentlemen, *"Does he mean, Wilson Jr. High School and Franklin High School Mr. Ben Nix?"*

The older gentlemen smiled at me and said, *"Yes. And who am I talking to?"*

I said to him, *"Ken Bordeaux."*

He gave me a big smile and said, *"I thought you looked familiar."*

Mr. Nix and I chatted for awhile bringing up old times. You see, Mr. Nix was a Junior and Senior High School Physical Education teacher and coach for many years in Rochester. He was my 7th, 8th and part of my 9th grade gym teacher; but more importantly, he was my 7th and 8th grade baseball coach which is a perfect segway into what I want to talk to you about in this chapter.

One evening in the 8th grade at baseball practice, Mr. Nix was working with the infield ball players while I and the other outfield players were warming up throwing the ball around. When he finished warming up the infield, he started hitting pop fly balls into the outfield. I must have been pretty decent player because I remember practicing in the left field. Mr. Nix hit a pop fly out to me. I ran up underneath the ball. When the ball came down, all I remember is that the right side of my left hand reeked with pain and I immediately shook my glove off and fell to the ground holding my left hand between my legs. Mr. Nix ran out to the outfield and checked my hand. My hand was very red and throbbing.

He looked at me and said, *"You tried to catch the ball in the wrong way. You are not supposed to catch the ball in the pocket, but in the web."*

He was right. This hurt very badly because I caught the ball wrong. I went home after practice with ice on my hand only to later find out that I had broken my left thumb.

As you can imagine, I had a good time of bringing that old story up to him while he waited for his chicken dinner order with his wife.

The point that I am trying to make here by using the incident with Mr. Nix is that coaches are not only for correction, but also for instruction. I never again caught a baseball in the pocket of my glove, but always in the web.

I went on to tell Mr. Nix that all the years I have played sports that would be the only time in my life that I have ever broken a bone.

If Coach Nix's instruction did not do anything for me, it taught me to do things the proper way in sports or suffer unnecessary consequences.

So it is in our spiritual walk. We can see the Apostle Paul in the verse at the beginning of the chapter using instruction to the church in Thessalonica. He is referencing the instructions that he had given them on living in Christ. Paul recognizes the instructions he gave were great for the church to adhere to so the people would live lives to please God.

The church in Thessalonica was a new church and they were learning the principles of the kingdom of God; therefore, they needed instructions.

The people in Thessalonica had adopted the instructions that the Apostle Paul had given them. They were living lives that were pleasing to God. Isn't it amazing how good instructions are for the sole purpose of keeping us out of error? A good coach in your life will help you stay out of trouble. We all can use people in our lives that keep us from trouble. I find myself conducting that role much in the lives of young believers. They do not need an entire dissertation of the Bible. They are already familiar with the word of God. They just need someone to coach them through life's difficulties and battles as they are trying to adjust to their new life in Christ.

I realize that regardless of what I have been through in my own life, I do have more than 30years of Christian experience. That is more than enough years to coach someone through life's storms.

We must recognize that the instructions that the church of Thessalonica had received were not day-to-day instructions given by man. They were instructions given to them by the Apostle Paul through the authority of Jesus.

Many times we are given instructions, but we do not recognize the authority behind them. I cannot begin to tell you the amount of times that I had given someone instruction, but because they did not recognize the authority behind what I said, they are now paying the price for not listening.

I learned many years ago not to be concerned about the response to an instruction I given another person. It is like being a mail carrier.

All I can do is deliver the mail. If a person adheres to it or not, I cannot be concerned.

We are living in a time when there are so many people who do not follow a coach's instruction.

Now, let's go back to my conversation with Mr. Nix in the chicken restaurant. I remember telling him that I had also taken up coaching and had been doing so for 18 years. Along with that, I told him that I had also attended college and received my degree in Computer Information Systems Management. I told him that even though sometimes we were knuckle-heads, I wanted him to know that his labor was not in vain. I received something from his teaching and leadership.

Mr. Nix said, "*Oh no, back then—you guys listened. These kids today don't listen to nobody.*" He only confirmed what I have been saying all along.

I am very concerned about our youth of today. Many of them really have a hard time receiving instruction. They are going after life with no direction. It is as if the more defiant they can be, the better they feel.

Unfortunately, a lot of the problems these youth face do not originate within themselves. They get the idea from having witnessed too many adults conduct themselves in the same kind of rebellious manner.

I thank God that people like Mr. Nix have been in my life. The same disciplined and insightful character that he coached many of us kids with was the same leadership that was apparent when I saw him that night in the restaurant 35 years later.

That night, I realized just how much I listened to the instruction of my coaches. I have a lot to thank them all for even until this day.

CHAPTER 4

A Coach for Encouragement

Paul sent for the disciples and, after encouraging them, said good-by and set out for Macedonia.

He traveled through that area, speaking many words of encouragement to the people.

~Acts 20:2

I sat quietly and resting in the aisle seat on an airplane next to a young lady. She slightly nudged me and asked if she could get up to go to the rest room.

I stood up in the aisle of the plane to let her out. As I sat back down, I could not but notice the title of the book she had been reading: *"Prozac Nation"* by Elizabeth Wurtzel. I wondered if this young lady was suffering from any form of depression or was she just reading this book for information. I did not know.

My spirit was drawn towards her after I read the title of the book for two reasons: she was very young, young enough to be my daughter and secondly, I had firsthand experience with a woman suffering from depression. The experience was unlike anything I had ever encountered. Because of this, I had done some research and study on anxiety, depression and mental disorder. According to the National Institute of Mental Health (NIMH),an estimated 26.2 percent of Americans ages 18 and older—about one in four -suffer from diagnosable mental disorder in a given year.[6]

6   2008,NIMH, Chapman and Perry, *Preventing Chronic Disease, Volume 5, No. 1, January 2008*

The NIMH also reported that by 2020, depression will only be second to heart disease. I came to realize that people suffering from depression are quietly growing culture within our society that most of us are not aware of.

Now back to my airline story. When the young lady returned, I let her back in her seat. I could tell that she had become aware that I had taken notice of the subject of her book, but she did not comment about it. She sat back in her seat and I leaned back and began to rest.

As I drifted off into rest again, several minutes later, I heard someone sobbing. I looked up. The young lady seated next to me was crying. Still not sure how old she was, I asked:

"Ma'am, are you alright?"

There was no answer. Again, I asked her, *"Ma'am, are you alright?"*

Again, there was no answer.

I asked one more time,

"Ma'am, are you alright?"

She looked up at me and said she was ok. I realized that God was opening a door for me to talk with her. What she needed, I knew, was residing within me.

I had been teaching a series at church entitled: *"How to Have a Prosperous Spirit, Soul and Body."* It was clear to me that this young lady's spirit was broken and her soul was emotionally off kilter.

The young lady and I spoke together for awhile. In the midst of our conversation, I realized that she did not need a father, friend or pastor. What she needed was a coach. She needed some spiritual information that made sense to her and she could understand.

I recognized that this was an extremely bright, inteligent, and educated young lady. She just lacked knowledge about herself. She was 23 years old, young enough to be my daughter as I thought, and a music writer.

She was in desperate need of encouragement. I recognized that we were on two totally different spiritual levels. Instead of preaching to her, I coached her.

She clearly had the ability to gather information, process it quickly, and recognize what was going on with her. In the world we live in today, there is nothing like knowing or meeting someone who can encourage you.

Regardless of all the scientific and technological advancements that have been made in our society, there is still a sense of more profound sadness in people than ever before. It seems the more knowledge that we possess, the sadder we become. We all can use coaches for encouragement in our lives. Notice that I said coaches, not a coach. From what I have seen and experienced, I believe we all need more than one coach. Life has so many peaks, turns, and valleys that you will never know when you are going to need someone to coach and encourage you through a situation.

The Apostle Paul knew the power of encouragement. He never missed an opportunity to encourage the saints. He was the "Apostle" of all Apostles, yet he much rather encourage the people more than anyone. He was the point man for the church. He was the leader, the coach. Good coaches know when to encourage and when not to.

Although Paul had the authority to correct, rebuke and instruct—encouraging was also in his power. Life is about balance. Unfortunately, our society is becoming much more sensitive than it's ever has been. People only want to be told what is good about them and not what they are doing that is wrong and unpleasant. We must realize that encouragement must have balance. If you are always told great things about yourself, one will never address your flaws. With that being said, I believe that encouragement is a much needed spirit in society. It has its value and rewards.

As I write this, I am reminded of a dilemma I noticed on our 2006 semi-professional football team. The owners and head coaches of the team had done something that many of the other teams in the league were not willing to do. They had purposely and aggressively recruited younger and less experienced talent to try out for the team.

In semi-professional football, it is common for coaches to recruit veteran ball players to get as much experience as possible. They recognize that the veterans have the skill level that can immediately advance them into post-season play. Our team had done a combination of recruiting veteran and rookie athletes. Our younger athletes struggled a lot. I noticed that when the coaches would pull the rookies out of the game, it was more like punishment then correction. The coaches did not communicate to the player what they had been doing wrong that prevented the team from executing a play. Because of this approach, I noticed that the morale of these talented young players kept going down.

I was the wide receiver coach, and my style was a little different from some of the other coaches when it came to dealing with players. I made it clear in practice what I expected on game day. When a player was not meeting my expectations during a game, I could easily address it, get him to correct it, or put in another player who was willing to meet the expectations. The players knew what I expected. They did not always like it, but they knew what I expected.

I had challenged some of our coaches to not just take these young players out of the game without communicating to them what they were doing wrong and what was expected of them. I wanted them to truly coach them and not just play them in the games. Our young players had a lot of issues and it carried over into their performance during games.

There was a lot to deal with, but they all had great talent and were very coachable. This meant that the coaches would have to get to know these players better. In order to encourage someone, you have to get to know them. That means you have to take a valid interest in their life. Our coaches began to do just that and we got great results from our players in post-season play. We won the overall championship for the state of Colorado.

The word "encourage" means to inspire with courage, spirit, or confidence, to stimulate by assistance, to promote, advance or foster.[7]

Living a Christian life requires a great deal of encouragement. In fact, believers are admonished in Hebrews 10:25:

> *"Let us not give up meeting together, as some are in the habit of doing, but let us encourage one another—and all the more as you see the Day approaching."*

---

7   *Merriam-Webster On-Line Dictionary*

In order to encourage or be encouraged, you need people in your life who you meet or greet regularly. No person, coach or leader can always be there daily to encourage any of us. That is why I believe you should have more than one encouraging person in your life. I truly do believe in this approach towards life. I keep encouraging people in my life, whether near or far. With today's advanced technology, this is very easy to do. All it takes is a phone call, email, video clips, books, tapes, CDs, text messaging, Facebook, Twitter or Skype chat.

If you expect to be encouraged, you must be encouraging yourself. In this life you can get back what you put out. Never in my life have I been lacking in encouragement. Since I was a child, I have always encouraged so many people. Also, I have learned to encourage those who want to be encouraged. That way you do not waste time.

You can spend a lot of time encouraging those who really do not desire your counsel, "*Do not throw your pearls to swine*" *(Matthew 7:6b)*. Know the difference and do not waste valuable time. We all will get back what we put out. We need encouraging people in our lives today.

Depression is on the rise. Anxiety is at an all-time high. Prozac, Zoloft and Abilifyare flying off the shelves. I have no idea what people are doing to become so depressed. All I can tell you is that we all have bad seasons and hard times, but none of it is worth depression and suicide.

This is why you need encouraging material, coaches, and people accessible to you. Do not fret and do not stall, be an encourager and get the encouragement that you need today. The word of God is always a great place to start. It has been my encouragement resource for the past 30 years. You never have to look for it. It is always near you.

CHAPTER 5

A Coach to Keep You from Quitting

"Let us not become weary in doing well, for at the proper time we will reap a harvest if we do not give up."

~Galatians 6:9

Out of all the chapters that I can write on in this book, this is bar-none the most important that can be discussed. At the time of this writing, America is facing one of its greatest economic challenges since the *"Great Depression."* Jobs are being lost by the hundreds of thousands each month.[8]

Barack Obama, the 44th President of the United States of America and his White House staff has inherited an American crisis which warrants immediate and swift changes to get our economy growing again.

There is very little to no international trade. Just about every industry has an overstock of supplies, but very little demand since business and banks are holding on to their money. In the meantime, many people are wondering how they are going to do to pay their bills, mortgages, cars, medical expenses, school loans, or business loans. If ever there was a time in history America and the world at large need some encouragement to keep from quitting, the time is now!

Barack Obama won the presidential elections by campaigning on a message of hope and change to a desperately failing society. For the first time in a long time, every American has been affected in some

8   *Washington Post Staff Writers Saturday, Feb 7, 2009*

way or the other by the same financial issues. Bernard Madoff only added insult to injury by being discovered to have ripped off nearly $50 billion of American investor's dollars in the one of largest "*Ponzi*" schemes in the nation's history. This scheme lasted at least 25 years and the government had to go after over $170 billion dollars from Mr. Madoff 's assets. Even though his charges added up to 150 years in prison, thousands of people lost the bulk of their retirement and pension plans. Included in these losses were the assets of 35 labor unions. We have seen countless lay-offs and home foreclosures, CEO's and banks have been accused of misusing federal government bail-out money, homeless shelters are over crowded, and the development of tent cities is on the rise. There has been an increase in the high school dropout rates. The suicide rate has also increased. So have the incidents of individuals walking into various public places and killing people randomly.

The fact of the matter is that many people have given up on life. Again, if there was ever a time that we needed a coach to encourage us not to give up, the time has arrived. When coaching kids and adults for the past 20 years, one of the basic elements we teach is to *"never ever quit."*

When a person quits, various elements begin to manifest in their being that affects the whole person and the entire team. Doubt, cynicism, negative emotional behavior, the poisoning of others' spirits, hopelessness and the like begin to creep in. These traits are no more than signs of a person *"giving up"* or *"quitting."*

I never liked quitting and do not have too much room in my heart for a quitting spirit. Quitters can be destructive. They can tear up faster than you can build. When we quit, we not only are affecting ourselves, but we infect others around us.

The unfortunate thing I have learned about those who quit is they do not care at the time who they are affecting. Our American society has reflected this not only in our homes, but in our economic, healthcare, educational and financial systems.

I like what President Obama said in his speech on education reform to the students. He said:

"If you are a student listening, do not even think about dropping out of school. It's not an option. Quitting school is not only giving up on yourself, but your country as well.[9]

Life is about perseverance. Nothing is ever gained in this life when we stop investing in ourselves educationally. We are all guaranteed to face adversity and difficult times. If we do not have someone in our lives to teach us not to give up, we will do just that—quit!

How many of us who been involved in any form of athletics had coaches who pushed us when we were ready to give up? The purpose of their pushing us was not to hurt us, but to teach us what it takes to have a chance at winning. Even if you never participated in a sport, the same principle applies to us all.

When I was in 2nd grade, I remember my mother enrolling myself, my oldest brother, and my little sister in a Catholic School in Rochester, New York—Immaculate Conception. My second oldest brother's third grade class was full and he had to attend a public school that was directly across the street from ours.

Like a lot of children, I tended to struggle in different areas of learning. I had difficulty in reading and writing. I remember how difficult it was for me to not only read, but comprehend what I was reading. I can remember how I struggled with knowing what time it was on a simple clock.

There were many times my teacher would work with me after school. Even though I worked hard, I struggled. But it would be the teachers and Nuns at my school who would work with me and encourage me not to quit, not to give up, to keep working hard.

I tried to win classroom contests for prizes and would always fall short. Although this hurt not to win a prize, I kept working hard. I particularly remember my teachers, Ms. Madeline, Ms. Weathers, and the unforgettable Sister Jean, whom the kids called, *"Sister Mean Jean."* These women were my coaches in the classroom. They pushed me and would not let me quit.

There were others, Mr. Smalls, Mr. Carter, Sister Barbara Fox, Sister Matilda, and Father Brennan. All of these teachers, in different

---

9   *Education Reform: http://www.cnn.com Live March 10, 2009*

ways, pushed me to continue to work hard and learn. It was hard, but everything they did helped me and encouraged me to keep trying.

I was placed in remedial reading programs to help me with my reading and comprehension. In those days, they put a pair of headsets on you and you read along with an audio tape and then answered questions.

I found that my problem was not being able to block out additional noise that got my attention. The headsets worked wonderfully for me. Also, the repetition of doing this over and over taught me how to concentrate. These are the things that good coaches and leaders discover about us. They locate and help solve the problems within us.

It was a long road, it did not get fixed over night, but it got fixed. I realize now that my problem back then was the ability to focus and concentrate on what I was reading. Whatever the problem was, I was taught not to quit. To be honest with you, my reading issues did not get solved until after high school while I was in the Air Force my first year. I still had to take extra reading instructions.

For what it is worth, I became conditioned to people who taught me not to quit. It is these kinds of people I have developed such a great appreciation, love and respect for because they were right. You never gain anything by quitting. For example, I was once being pressured by a certain person to quit college when I only had three months left from graduation. I thought what I was going through was crazy even though the pressure was real and intense. I thank God that my dad, who was in his last months of battling with lung cancer, called me and said that he had sought his doctor's permission to come to Colorado and see me graduate. That was enough to seal the deal for me to not quit. Dad's doctor had given him the go ahead to come and my father flew out to watch me graduate. The next day, my Pastor at the time surprised me and licensed me in the ministry at church. Little did I know at the time that my father had just five months to live. I am so glad that I did not give in to the pressure from another person to quit school. It did not make sense. If I had done that, my father would not have seen his only son graduate from college and get licensed in the ministry. That was one of the proudest weekends of Dad's life. He got to see both ceremonies. People who never finished anything in their life are always the first ones to try to get you to quit what you are doing. Do not do it. Unless the Lord tells you to stop, do not ever quit.

Can you imagine how I would have felt if I had come that far in a 4 year degree program, only to quit with three to four months left? Thank God that I stayed and finished. The Apostle Paul said *"Let us not become weary in doing well, for at the proper time we will reap a harvest if we do not give up" (Galatians 6:9)*. We must realize the harvest does not come to those who quit; it only comes to those who persevere.

Many times, if you are not careful, you will find yourself involved with those who do not mind giving up on things. In order to achieve something in your life, you may have to reconsider your relationships—all of them. Bad relationships will inevitably weigh on your spirit.

If you do not have a quitting spirit, separate yourself from those who do. It will be a matter of life and success of your accomplishments. This will be my third book that goes to print. Trust me, it does not happen by giving up. No one wants to live life and not succeed. Success always comes at a price. Quitting cannot be a part of the equation.

I have had good natural and spiritual leadership in my life who encouraged me to never give up. So often we give up on ourselves. I see it more than I would like to. I want to encourage you to surround yourself with those who never give up and glean from those who admonish you to do the same.

CHAPTER 6

A Coach to Learn How to Get Over a Loss

"But this one thing I do, forgetting those things which are behind, and reaching forth unto those things which are before."

~Philippians 3:13

One of the traps I have noticed in my 20 years of coaching is that many leaders are so focused on winning, they never teach their players how to get over a loss. It is not only in sports that we have this problem, but it's in every aspect of life. In my short 50 years on this earth, I have learned that losing is a part of life. No one wins every time. We will all, if we live long enough, suffer loss more than once. If we look at what has been going on in our American economy, many people who did the right thing, saved their money, invested in stock and business, found themselves watching their portfolios and retirement plans become worth little or nothing. We are reeling from the fact that others who knew better, took money which did not belong to them and make bad investments all in the spirit of greed.

Loss is something that we all experience. It cuts across race, color, sex, religion and cultural status. When I was 29 years old, I lost my father. My father finally lost his fight with lung cancer and died. If you asked me, it was during a time that I felt I needed my dad most. I was young, raising a family, two children, and one on the way. My father was more experienced in marriage and family matters than myself. I looked to his wisdom on how to deal with a wife and children. All these things and more I confided in him, so his loss was a grievous one for me. I was a man, and the man who was helping me understand what it meant to be a man had just died.

I wasn't ready for this loss. It came too soon. That's how loss is in our lives. Many times we are not ready for it, but it shows up anyway. This point drives me to the purpose for why I am writing about learning to get over a loss. If we do not have quality skills to get over these losses in our lives, we can spend precious years in a dark hole of misery.

When King David's first born was dying after his affair with Bathsheba, he did something amazing when the child was dead. I am not sure if King David had been taught how to get over loss or if all great people know something that most common folk do not understand. Whatever he understood, I believe his story can serve a purpose to gain insight on what we should do when you lose something or someone. The story reads:

> *After Nathan had gone home, the Lord struck the child that Uriah's wife had borne to David, and he became ill. David pleaded with God for the child. He fasted and went into his house and spent the nights lying on the ground. The elders of his household stood beside him to get him up from the ground, but he refused, and he would not eat any food with them. On the seventh day the child died. David's servants were afraid to tell him that the child was dead, for they thought, "While the child was still living, we spoke to David but he would not listen to us. How can we tell him the child is dead? He may do something desperate." David noticed that his servants were whispering among themselves and he realized the child was dead. "Is the child dead?" he asked. "Yes," they replied, "he is dead." Then David got up from the ground. After he had washed, put on lotions and changed his clothes, he went into the house of the Lord and worshiped. Then he went to his own house, and at his request they served him food, and he ate. His servants asked him, "Why are you acting this way? While the child was alive, you fasted and wept, but now that the child is*

dead, you get up and eat!" He answered, "While the child was still alive, I fasted and wept. I thought, 'Who knows? The Lord may be gracious to me and let the child live.' But now that he is dead, why should I fast? Can I bring him back again? I will go to him, but he will not return to me." Then David comforted his wife Bathsheba, and he went to her and lay with her. She gave birth to a son, and they named him Solomon. The Lord loved him;[10]

If you read this story well, you will see that David was in a very grieved state while his son was dying. When he learned that the child was dead, his entire attitude changed almost immediately. I have read this text time after time and I have always thought that the King acted strangely. But what I learned from reading this is a principle of the kingdom that we all must understand. We must all learn to get over losses and get over them fast. The sooner you get over it, the better. Grieve it, mourn it, and get over it. I have since taught my kids who I coached in youth football, and the young men in the adult league, the same thing. In fact, I taught the children to get over a loss of a game within 72 hours and my adult players even sooner, 48 hours. The longer you hang on to a loss, the more time you waste not preparing for what is next. I found in football that teams who can get over a loss quickly are ready to go to practice the following week and do better the next game. Teams that argue, fret, and fight about last week's loss continue to lose over and over again. I coached successful winning teams with boys and men due to this one kingdom principle.

It is the same thing with a marriage. People, who hang on to old issues and never let them go, only set their marriage up for continual losses. These people never have closure on anything. Everything remains open to show their discontentment. Understand what I am talking about has to do with losing loved ones, jobs, marriages, children, friends, business deals, etc. I know that these are more precious than a game. I will never teach anyone to try to get over any loss of this nature within 48 to 72 hours, but the same principle applies. You have to get over your losses quickly. The sooner the better for you and everyone that is connected to you. The thing that grieves me about American culture is that we are not a culture that allows and respect one's time

---

10   *2 Samuel 12:15-24*

for mourning. In our culture, it does not matter if you lose a parent or loved one, many bosses still want you to come back to work ready to go in three days. Unfortunately, that is not good for anybody. It's not good for the person who has experienced the loss, the customer, or the employer.In Jewish society, if a person loses a parent, they are allowed up to one year to mourn. After that year, they move on with life. The entire community respects and recognizes their mourning season. There is a start date and an end date. That is what counts.[11] When we experience loss in our lives we have to learn how to put it behind us as soon as we can. Getting on with life is more important than stewing over what is dead. My oldest brother lost his youngest son to an early death just a few years ago. I watched him struggle for the first year or so when his son was gone. Since then, he picked up the pieces and moved on with his life. I say that to say this, I rather be hurt, disappointed and moving on with life; than broken, battered, bruised, and not going anywhere. My mother and uncle did not raise us that way and thank God they did not. I see so many people who become as Pastor George Aja says:

"Stuck in a rut with a skunk in a bunk."

We cannot afford to do this in our lives. We have to get over the losses we experience as soon as possible. You need people and coaches to teach you how to lose just as much as how to win. This is the proper way to lose in life, get over it quick. It is not losing that is important, it is how we move on from it. No one in their right mind wants to lose, but when it happens, you know how to get over it and get over it sooner than later. If we take a little advice from the Apostle Paul, who had experienced a great deal more than any of us, he learned to *"forget those things that be behind and reach forth to those things which are before."*[12]. This is a powerful statement which deserves our attention. There is so much opportunity in life. There is so much that is before us. Why waste our time worrying about a loss that happened in your past? I say your past because that is where it is, in your past. It is only present if you keep it there. I know that this is easier said than done, but it is possible. People do it all the time. Every day under the sun, people get over losses. Paul clearly was one who was able to do it through Christ. I

---

11   *Jewish Mourning Laws – Jewish Center for Jewish Christian Relations*
12   *Philippians 3:13*

have overcome plenty in my worst seasons of life. Why? I refuse to get *"stuck in a rut, with a skunk in my bunk."* We all have our lives to live which will be accountable to the Master when our day is done. Get on with your life. The bigger the loss, the greater your revelation of God will be and greater the harvest of blessing for you. I will leave you with this poem my sister sent to me years ago when I was going through my greatest storm.

> *"Prepare yourself to accept your pain as purpose, while practicing the power of patience to prevail." If you want to get something you never had, you have to do something you never done. When God allows something to be taken from your grasp, He's not punishing you, but merely opening your hands to receive something better. 'The will of God will never take you where the Grace of God will not protect you.' Something good will happen to you today; something that you have been waiting to hear...*
> *Author YL.*

In conclusion, never be afraid of losses because losses always leave you a gift...experience! Learn to lose and put the experience from it into practice.

CHAPTER 7

Importance of Being Coachable

"There was a man who had two sons. The younger one said to his father, 'Father, give me my share of the estate.' So he divided his property between them. Not long after that, the younger son got together all he had, set off for a distant country and there squandered his wealth in wild living. After he had spent everything, there was a severe famine in that whole country, and he began to be in need."

~Luke 15:11-14

When we look at the story of the prodigal young son, we see a young man who was very head strong. This young man went to his father to get all that belonged to him in the estate, then went off into riotous living. He spent all he had on parties, entertainment and prostitution. There was nothing this young man left himself to desire. For over two thousand years, this story has been one of the most popular stories ever preached in the church.[13] I believe this story is taught a lot because so many of us have identified with it. Either it was we ourselves, like the prodigal son, who had rebelled against our parents, or we know someone very close to us who has.

Rebellion against a parent or parents is like cancer, we all know someone who has it or had it at one time. We do not have to look far to get a good picture of it. For many, all you have to do is look in the mirror or in your house. All the years I have preached the gospel, I have never really delved a lot into this story. It is not because I did

---

13   *Luke 15:11-32*

not believe in its truth or I had no time to do so; for me, I believe it has been because the Spirit of God has never really given me much revelation on it than it clearly states.

Interesting enough, when preparing to write on the subject in this chapter, this is the story that came to mind with deep revelation into its content. Like you, I always seen the prodigal son as a young man who was rebellious against his father. As I look more spiritually into the text, this young man was something that I am fully aware of as a coach, but never saw it in this story. This young man was not coachable. He was unteachable. I know from personal coaching experience, when you have a player who is not coachable, you are going to have a very riotous, out of control, self-centered, disruptive person to deal with. In the life of coaching, we coaches are always looking for the guy or gal that is coachable. Someone who cooperates with the goal is what we want. Why? It is because our experience teaches us that you can get more done at practice, and will accomplish your objectives on game day, when you have players who are coachable.

We realize that non-coachable players take up your time and everyone's time on the team. They are always and clearly counterproductive to the whole of the organization. A person who is not coachable whines more than they produce. For instance, look at some of the "whiners" in the National Football League (NFL) and National Basketball Association (NBA). You know who they are; I do not have to name names. How much productive time has been stolen by their whining, crying and bellyaching over trivial matters like: *"I am not getting the ball enough,"* or *I am not getting enough playing time.* "When I played football and basketball in high school, I received more pleasure from blocking for our running backs or getting the ball to our best shooter on the team. If you tackled my best friend on the football team too many times, I made sure you thought twice about running up on him again. Coachable people think about the big picture and not about themselves.

Many of these hard to deal with players go from team to team. They rarely find anybody that can coach them. In the end, the entire organization winds up suffering from having them as part of the team. To be honest with you, they are lethal in your locker rooms and team meetings. Now that they have cell phones, text messaging, and sports interviews, they are even more dangerous. The worse thing you can give these kinds of players is some kind of media-outlet. The same applies for those of us who in everyday life who are not coachable. You create more bad than good. NFL and NBA teams have found that sometimes you have to release people out of their contract. Let them go. Get rid of them!

The truth of this matter is in the story that Jesus told the people about the prodigal son. It was not so much that this boy was rebellious, but it was more so that he was too heady, self-centered, disobedient, and out-of-control. He had a lot of his own flesh to burn off. He did not care who he walked over. No one could talk to him, no one could teach him, no one could reach him, and neither could anyone coach him. His rebellion was a manifestation of what he felt he already knew. To him, he understood not only more than his father, but also his older brother. Notice that the older brother does everything that his father had ever commanded him to do. He was always taken care of and in his dad's graces. It was the younger who did the opposite because he was clearly un-teachable.

To be un-coachable means to be unteachable. Coaching is nothing more than being able to point a person or a team in the right direction. When we look at College Basketball players, I think of the *Duke Blue Devils*. Since 1980, their most respected and prolific coach, Mike Krzyzewski, has been able to teach top basketball recruits from all over the country. In ten different seasons, he placed the *Blue Devils* in a position to win a *NCAA-Final Four Men's Basketball Championship*. When I look at the *NCAA Men's College Football*, it has been coach Urban Meyer who *Florida Gators* have won two *National BCS Title Championships* in the past four years. He is the only coach in the history of the *South Eastern Conference* (SEC) to win two outright national titles.

My point is that coaches who find players who are coachable, do consistently better then coaches who do not have such luck. The young prodigal son more than likely did more to harm his father's business and land then he did to help. He had an attitude of defiance because he felt that he knew more about how to live than his dad. This is a mistake a lot of young people make today. The young son set out to prove to his older brother and father that he knew more and would live a better life than both of them. Because of his riotous mindset, he found himself completely broke, distressed, and dysfunctional. To make matters worse, the country started experiencing a famine. Now he was out of money, food, shelter and support. Things had gotten so bad for him that he had to sell himself off as a hired servant or slave just to get by. He noticed that even the pigs that he took care of were eating better than him.

How deplorable of a position to find yourself in all because you are un-coachable. Normally, when no one can teach you anything, you will find yourself in these kinds of grave positions. God gives us people in our lives to teach, coach, and train us. It is the experiences we get with the people that He assigns to us that we need to pay most attention. They are slated to serve a God-given purpose in our lives. Too many are going without their God ordained coaches to help get them from point A to point B in life. The young son thought he could do it all alone and did not realize that God had already ordained his father and his older brother to help him develop into a successful young man. The good thing about this story is at least the oldest son had paid much attention to his father. The father would have had a bigger mess on his hands if both sons had done the same thing. One son was wise and the other son was foolish.

Somewhere in the past 20 to 30 years, young people have started going their own way. They are like headless horse-man, running amuck not knowing where they are going. The coaches that guide them are instruments of gangs, violence, rock-n-roll, gangster rappers, and satanic influences. They are misguided rockets ready to hit innocent bystanders with their reckless thinking. It will only be when they destroy too much that they will realize the destruction they became apart of was not worth it. As one woman said to me, "they are lost." Many are in a great need to become coachable. No one person can lead him or herself. We all need voices in our lives that help direct our lives. The lack of being coachable has drawn a great wedge between the older and younger generations. We are admonished in scripture that the younger men and women are to learn from the older men and women. In the book 1 Peter 5:5, it say's " *Young men are to be submissive to those who are older."* Titus 2:3-4 says the older women are to be *"reverent in the way they live, not to be slanders or addicted to much wine, but to teach what is good. Then they can train the younger women to love their husbands and children."* With the respect to society and the desire for change, there are some things we should not stop doing. One of those things is the teacher—stu-dent relationship between older men and younger men and older women and younger women. If it has worked in the past, why go to something that does not work and leaves our young people lost?

Prayerfully, young people today can once again find the need for the seasoned leaders in their lives. The desire to pull away from people of understanding has been too extreme in this country. This has been wrong and has not born any good fruit. We need to go back to being a nation where we put our foot down on a children being teachable and respectful to the older generation. This new age philosophy that teaches students in our schools that they do not have to follow their parents teachings is satanic, demonic, and of the devil. I was pleased to witness Barack Obama understand the importance of coaches, advisors, and leaders in his life. He understood it so much that it led him all the way to the highest seat as President of the United States.

When you talk to great leaders, they will always mention to you the many voices, including older people, they learned from in their lives. This itch to say whose advice matters, and who's does not, is a grave mistake that many people make. Everyone has something that you can take from them that is worthy of investigation. Rebellion is a spirit and it has caused our young people to be untrainable; and therefore, misguided. The scriptures teach:

> *"For rebellion is as the sin of witchcraft, and stubbornness
> is as of iniquity and idolatry."*[14]

There is a lot of rebellion in our young generation today. Like the prodigal son, the young must return to their senses and become coachable before it is too late.

---

14   *1 Samuel 15:23*

CHAPTER 8

Acknowledge You Need a Coach

"Paul, an apostle of Christ Jesus by the command of God our Savior and of Christ Jesus our hope, To Timothy my true son in the faith. "

~ 1 Timothy 1:1-2

In the previous chapter we talked about being coachable. We must understand a person will never be coachable if they do not take the time to realize that they need a coach. You will never ask or look for what you do not discern that you need. There was a time when people knew that in order to get to their desired destination, they would need someone who knows more than they do to help them. If we focus on the subject of life, very few people today are looking for coaches who can lead them to have life. The reason for the lack of this pursuit in today's society is because many have not recognized that they need this kind of leadership in their lives. Simply this, if you do not think you need a coach, you will never look for one. When we look at Paul and Timothy's relationship in the Bible, we see Timothy submitting himself to the Apostle Paul as a *"true son."*[15] Let me make it clear to you that Paul and Timothy were not related, but Paul saw him as true son in the gospel after observing how well Timothy took to him and learned from him. Timothy, to his credit, recognized that he could not advance in the work of the kingdom of God without a leader or mentor like Paul. Realizing this, Timothy submitted his spirit, soul, and body to Paul in learning how to build the church. This gives us an indication of what a person is like who recognizes that he needs a coach. He or she

15   1 Timothy 1:2

will become more like a son or daughter to the person who is teaching them.If we look at the life of Naomi and Ruth we see the same type of relationship between a mother-in-law and daughter-in-law. After the death of her husband, Naomi's son, Ruth insisted on staying and taking care of her mother-in-law. She refused to return home to her native land even though Naomi encouraged her to do so. Ruth refused her mother-in-laws encouragement and stayed at Naomi's side and the two of them went back to Naomi's home in Moab. The Lord showed favor to Ruth. She ended up marrying a very wealthy man named Boaz. She became pregnant and gave Naomi a grandson. Boaz noticed the love that Ruth had for her mother-in-law and said to Naomi:

> *"For your daughter-in-law, who loves you and who is better to you than seven sons."*[16]

In those days, a son's faithfulness and love towards his mother and father was highly recognized and respected. Here we see Ruth's love for her mother-in-law being compared as better than not one son, but seven sons. That was a huge statement for Boaz to make in a society that thought so much more of the birth of a male over a female. He knew that Ruth was a great woman based on how well she took care of Naomi and stood by her side. That kind of love and commitment made Boaz fall in love with Ruth and want to marry her.Looking at this story more carefully, we see the outcome of Naomi's life was great because she was willing to listen, learn, and be coached by her mother-in-law. The two of them returned to the country of Moab without anything to show for the years they were away. When Ruth realized that Naomi met Boaz, who was a distant relative of hers, she considered an idea that could potentially bless her daughter-in-law. The Bible states:

> *"One day Naomi her mother-in-law said to her, "My daughter, should I not try to find a home for you, where you will be well provided for? Is not Boaz, with whose servant girls you have been, a kinsman of ours? Tonight he will be winnowing barley on the threshing floor. Wash and perfume yourself, and put on your best clothes. Then go down to the threshing floor, but do not let him know you are there until he has finished eating and drinking. When he lies down, note the place where he is lying. Then*

16   *Ruth 4:15.*

go and uncover his feet and lie down. He will tell you what
to do." "I will do whatever you say," Ruth answered.[17]

Boaz was a righteous man who knew the man who should be first in line to redeem Naomi and her daughter-in-law. He spoke with him at the town gate to see if he would do so. The man refused to do so; therefore, it left Boaz, being the next in line, the right to redeem Naomi. He would then marry Ruth. In this story, Ruth gets the blessing of listening to the instructions of her mother-in-law who was teaching her how to be a woman. We should really consider what the Apostle Paul wrote:

"And we know that in all things, God works for the good
of those who love him, who have been called according to
his purpose."[18]

If this did not work for the good of both Naomi and Ruth, I do not know what could have. Unfortunately, in today's world, the call for ignorance and rebellion in the young people has stripped their desire to be led, coached, or taught by anybody. It seems like, if you do not look like Kanye West, 50 Cents, Little Wayne, P-Diddy, Lady Ga-Ga, BeYonce, Paris Hilton, Little Kim, Chris Brown, or Rhianna, to name a few, the younger generation do not want to hear anything you have to say. The young do not recognize that their parents, pastors, math, science, English and history teachers are the people that are their real coaches and will shape them for success for the rest of their lives. The very ones they reject are the ones they need to listen to.

As a young boy, I recognized that I needed a coach. In fact, we all do. I remember gravitating to older men who knew what they were talking about. I listened to their wisdom and took to heart their advice and counsel. This has been a practice I have had kept until this day. I remember listening to every word Mr. Brown used to say to all of us young kids. He was so wise then and is to this very day. To this day, I still seek his counsel if I need it. It was as if he always knew what you were thinking. He was a man who always had time to talk to young boys. It framed my life. It taught me what was important. I have had people in my life not give me credit for listening, but they did

17   *Ruth 3:1-5*
18   *Romans 8:28*

not know is that I always paid attention, especially to people who had something to say. In fact, I learned not to listen to nonsense. I repel nonsense and go the other way. I learned this from my coaches. The big void today in America is that adults do not have the relationships we know we should have with our young people. The younger generation is being pulled by the wrong voices, teachers, and coaches. I believe the young today have more access to adults who can talk to them about growing up, but many young folk are not interested in they have to say. They do not recognize the resources they have in their homes, churches, communities, schools, recreation centers and social networks. Unfortunately in today's society, unless someone is mixing a CD, dropping tracks, or selling millions of records, many kids are not interested in their wisdom. They really do feel like they know more than their elders. The crux of the matter is that we are having a crisis with this generation. There is a huge gap between what they expect and reality. Some say that many parents are giving them too much. I feel that it is normal to do all you can for your children to ensure that they have a good start in life; however, there is another paradigm that teaches them to go without so that they can appreciate and have real expectations. Unfortunately, the gap I spoke of is getting wider and wider. I thought of what this gap would look like in the spirit when touring the Royal Gorge near Canon City, Colorado. The width of the canyon is 50 feet (15 m) at its base and a few hundred feet at its top. Either way, you have a huge gap at the top or the bottom. We must understand that one day the young will be the leaders and decision makers in this nation. It is almost frightening to think of who these young people will be. If we really look at it, it may be creating the perfect storm for there to be no one who is taking real responsibility and making strong decisions. The young must recognize they too need a coach in this world; and H*ip-Hop* (or for a lot of rappers, "*His Slop*") is not the answer. We are at war in Afghanistan, there is a fight for the sovereignty in the Ukraine, America and Russia are at their lowest moments since the Cold War, Israel is under attack by rockets in a conflict with Hamas, the Iranian nuclear program is causing major concerns in the middle east, mass killings are occurring in China, commercial airlines are being targeted by rebels with surface-to-air missiles, and it looks like America is heading back to help keep peace in Iraq. With twenty-five percent of high school students across the nation not graduating, how will our future leaders function if our kids are not being properly trained and graduating from high school? Who will be our future leaders and decision makers? Education has always been a key to shaping the economic status and growth of any nation. What will America look like in the future? We need to be relentless in raising a generation that can lead, and not just follow. I thank God for entertainment, but we will still need senators, congressman, doctors, lawyers, engineers, scientist, computer professionals, economists, and other professionals. Being a leader is recognizing you still need coaching beyond the 12th grade. Finishing high school is just a start out the gate; you still have to run the entire race.

It seems like many hold their children to very low expectations when it comes to academia. It is killing us. If we are not going to hold our children to obtaining at least a high school diploma, then why are we having children?

CHAPTER 9

A Coach to Teach You How to Win

"See, I have delivered Jericho into your hands, along with its king and it's fighting men. March around the city once with all the armed men. Do this for six days. Have seven priests carry trumpets of rams' horns in front of the ark. On the seventh day, march around the city seven times, with the priests blowing the trumpets.

When you hear them sound a long blast on the trumpets, have all the people give a loud shout; then the wall of the city will collapse and the people will go up, every man straight in."

~Joshua 6:2-5

"Listen carefully. You are to set an ambush behind the city. Do not go very far from it. All of you be on the alert. I and all those with me will advance on the city, and when the men come out against us, as they did before, we will flee from them. They will pursue us until we have lured them away from the city, for they will say, 'They are running away from us as they did before.' So when we flee from them, you are to rise up from ambush and take the city. The Lord your God will give it into your hand. When you have taken the city, set it on fire. Do what the Lord has commanded.

See to it; you have my orders."

~Joshua 8:4-8

In a previous chapter I talked about needing a coach to learn how to get over a loss. I really do believe that is a rare, essential, and probably the most neglected gift that a coach can bring in your life.

But let us make no mistake about it, the most important purpose of having a coach is to learn how to win. I believe in this wholeheartedly. When I first started coaching youth in little league football, I found myself in a very interesting and difficult position. I was enlisted in the United States Air Force and my third duty assignment would land me about 7 miles from Camp David at an Army Base, Fort Ritchie, Maryland. Not only was I stationed out in the middle of the hills of Pennsylvania and Maryland, but there were only a handful of Air Force personnel on this predominately Army base.

One day while at work, another Air Force co-worker of mine asked me if I would help him coach the base recreational little league football team. I had only been stationed on the base about 3 months and was still very new to the base community. He told me the boys he would be coaching were 11 and 12 years old and that they had never won a game. It sounded like a good thing to do and I knew I needed to acclimate to my new surroundings. I gladly accepted the offer. There were a few other coaches he had on his staff. I worked with the players who played defense. As we coached those children, I soon learned why this team had never won a game. They were part of the local Pop-Warner league that had established teams in the area. The children who were on the teams off the base were very good. Their teams had continuity and longevity. The base team suffered in those areas because their parents were reassigned to different posts frequently.

Needless to say, that first year I helped with the children, we lost all seven games on our schedule. We were a laughing stock to the entire league. It was horrible; but I fell in love with the children, so I did not mind being one of their coaches. It was not what I was used to. When I played Pop-Warner, we were always in the championship. The most we ever lost was one game a year. Not only were we losing often with these children on the base team, but we were hard pressed to score a touchdown. Our team had four or five exceptional kids, but we needed to get the other kids up to speed in order to compete decently. It was a lot of work and it did not happen that year. The next football season came around and the head coach had some coaching staff problems; therefore, he asked me if I would help him again with the boys now 12 and 13 years old. This time he wanted me to assist in coaching the offense. I accepted, but this time on different terms. I told the head coach I would assist coaching the offense if he would agree with me that we were going to coach the youth in a way to score points and win at least one game for the kids and their parents. We were going to score points and guarantee the players and their parents that we will win at least one game that year. I felt that we as coaches owed them that much if we were going to have these children coming out to practice after school several nights each week. I knew from my prior Pop-Warner experience that it was important for the players to score points and win a game. I never believed in teaching anyone to lose. It was not how I was taught when I played for the 10th Ward Tigers in Rochester, New York, and I wanted to teach the same principles to these children. Winning is an attitude. Sometimes it works and sometimes you get disappointed, but the attitude still has to be there. The intent had to be to go out and win games, not just have a team in the league. I felt it was very important the coaches work hard to guarantee these kids the experience of a win. We all have to start somewhere; and for this team, one win was a milestone.

The head coach agreed with me, so we went to work that year with the same players that we had the previous year. We designed our offense around the athletic ability of our best player who was our running back named Lamont. Lamont was tall, sleek, confident, handsome, and fast. In fact, he was tall enough that I gave him an old winter dress coat I received from my dad that I could no longer wear. Lamont had flare, flash, style, and a great smile. The only thing he was missing was good coaching. I worked with Lamont on setting up his teammates to make good blocks for him. He was so used to doing things on his own.

We had a few other kids who were his friends who were pretty good, but I noticed they enjoyed picking on our worse player–Timmy. I saw how Timmy sat on the bus by himself and did not interact with the other players. He would come to practice, but had no interest in being there. The first thing I knew I needed to do was to get him, and kids like him, to feel apart of the team. I spoke to the better players and got them to stop berating their teammates. These better players could play, but had no life skills. They learned that if I saw them picking on their teammates, it would not go over well with me. This was a disease that I learned was happening while they were at school away from us coaches. I had to put a stop to it. It was killing our team performance.

This went on all season. It was a piece of work. As far as scoring, we found ways to shake our best player lose on punts, kick returns and from scrimmage on other teams that year; nevertheless, we were still not winning. We were at game five of a short seven game schedule and had not won a game. Our chances of winning a game as promised were looking bleaker. I refused to give up on my dream to have these boys get a taste of one victory. The head coach and other coaches were starting to feel the pressure from the parents on our promise that these boys would win at least one game that year.

At this time some of the other coaches, players, and parents began to think I was a little crazy and needed to give up my dream of a win; but, something in me just could not give up. In my mind, winning one game for these kids was only right. I would never want to take a group of boys and not show them how to win if that is what they wanted. My upbringing was hard. I knew what constant losing did to people. It kills your spirit. Now I was watching how defeat had crippled these players in their little minds to not believe in themselves. The way they would talk about themselves and each other was paralyzing for me. My spirit couldn't take it. I did not have that experience as a kid playing sports at all. My little league teams, whether it was baseball, football, or basketball won and won a lot. We played local and won. We traveled and won. It just did not make sense. Being in the playoffs or championship was routine. I knew a playoff or championship was a big stretch for these boys, but one win out of a seven game season I felt any team could do. As we prepared for our last two games of the season, I told Timmy that he was going to play more. I wanted him to get more motivated in practice. That next week, he showed up to practice early. He was different. He was very different. I noticed that he had a pair of old working gloves on, but he had cut the finger tips out on each glove. His little fingers were exposed to the cold and his face looked ready for war. I was shocked. All the players and coaches noticed the difference in him. Timmy practiced his little heart out that week. He was blocking on offense and making tackles on defense. I couldn't believe it. I told the kids that we had two weeks left to give their parents a win and that Timmy was going to start on both the offensive and defensive lines.

That Saturday we played our sixth game of the season; and this time, we were in a dog fight. Lamont was running all over the opposing team and Timmy was blocking and tackling as if his life depended on it. The game came down to the final minutes of the fourth quarter. All the parents were there. It was cold and the kids were playing with desperation. We were, for first time all season, ahead during the close of regulation and time was running out. The score was 13 to 12.

The other team was inside our 10 yard line with a little less than 2 minutes left in the game. All the boys on our team were anxious for a victory, but knew they were in trouble. If the other team scored, that would be it. Timmy had made several big tackles, blocks, and one fumble recovery that gave us the ball back during the game. He was very muddy, cold and wet, but did not let any of this bother him at all. The kid looked like he had been a little man at work in construction all day. The coaches agreed to keep him in the game on the defensive line.

With time running out, the coaches agreed to put Lamont and another kid on a linebacker blitz with Timmy playing nose guard on defense. You could see his little white fingers exposed from his cut up gloves. The other team snapped the ball, the linebacker blitz went into action, and the next thing we knew the ball was on the wet ground. A huge pile of kids dove in for the ball but we could not tell who had it. We saw Lamont and couple of our other players jump up and point that the ball was going our way, but the referees had not signaled that yet. Coaches and parents were jumping up and down screaming. We knew that this team was getting ready to score if we did not get the ball back.

The referees ran into the pile, pulling kids out right and left. We could see some of our players pointing again that the ball was ours. It seemed as if it took forever for the referees to decide whose ball it was. Our parents were getting very agitated. The coaches were holding back each other and players from running onto the field. The next thing we saw was the referee pointing his finger towards our goal post. Pandemonium broke out on the side lines. Everyone on our side went ballistic! We were jumping up and down in celebration, but we still did not know who had recovered the ball. Finally, from the bottom of the pile arose one of our smallest kids on the field, with his little fingers, face, and entire uniform all muddy hugging the football for dear life. It was Timmy, he had recovered his second fumble of the game to secure our first win. The parents and players could not contain their emotions when they saw who held the ball in his hands. The players ran out on the field and jumped on top of Timmy celebrating. We had to clear players and parents off the field. We kneeled down the ball a couple of times after the snap and won the game. This was our first win of the season and the first win for the organization in many years. You would have thought those boys had just won the *Super Bowl*. The excitement was unbelievable. When coaches begin to teach players to win, it can become contagious. We still had one game left for the season. We had kept our promise and it gave us momentum into the next week. We won that game as well. Success breeds success. Our team ended up winning their last two games of the season. At the awards banquet, we gave each kid their trophy. We gave out special accomplishment trophies as well. Everyone in the room knew that Lamont was our Most Valuable Player (MVP) for the year. He walked up to the front of the room with his great smile and little swagger to receive his award. All the parents and coaches were so proud of him. He really was an outstanding athlete. When I began to speak about the kid that would win the Most Improved Player (MIP) of the Year, it seemed as if every eye at the banquet began to tear up because they knew who I was talking about without mentioning his name. Timmy was announced as the winner of that award and the standing ovation that he received that day was unbelievable. I know it had to change his life. Here was a kid who was used to losing and being treated like nothing. He faced his challenges and turned them around. Now he was the most respected and appreciated kid on the team.

That day, I made a commitment that if I ever coached youth again, I would coach them to win and not to lose. It is so important for a child's self-image and esteem that he or she has some victories growing up. I coached another team briefly when I was reassigned in the military and moved to Gaithersburg, Maryland. After that I would not coach again until ten years later when I had two sons and they were old enough to start playing little league football. I started with children who were five and six years old and remained with them until they were fourteen years of age. I taught them to win. Because of the lesson in winning, our players had only one losing season. Every year we were in the playoffs; and one year, we were in the championship. I would never let my boys play for organizations that did not believe in teaching the players to win.

Why is all of this important? Because you need to understand coaches are in our lives to teach us to win. It does matter to kids to have some successes in life. Parents are only fooling themselves thinking that it does not matter. Children do not have to be the champions, but they do need to know the taste of victory, accomplishment, and what it takes to see their hard work rewarded. Hopefully, it will follow them for the rest of their lives. Not all kids are the same. Some learn from success and others do not. Winning, at least gives them an option. Again, it does not guarantee that they will always succeed in life, but it does give them something to look back on.

Let us look at the story of Joshua and his army as it relates to having a winning attitude. We see two distinct strategies God gave to Israel for them to win the war. Understand that in order to win anything, you need to have clear and distinct objectives. These objectives must be communicated and taught to those involved. Not everyone has the gift of coaching. It is a gift that comes from God, but you need cooperation for it to bear its fruit. Joshua had this special gift. Coaches in your life are the people who may have this gift of communication. Not everybody in your life should be coaching you. There are those who covet this gift, but have not waited patiently for it. True coaches normally have stories of success and accomplishment when they put their principles and training into practice. Winning should be the interest of the coach. No one gets anything out of losing all the time. Coaches know how to win and should know how to lose.

The Children of Israel marched up to Jericho under Joshua's command with only one objective in mind. They wanted to take over the city of Jericho and all of the land. They were to march around the city once for six days playing Jericho's death music and on the seventh day they were to do the same seven times. This was the strategy God gave to Joshua as to strike fear into the heart of their enemy. I am sure each day that Israel marched around the city of Jericho, more fear crept into the hearts and mind of the people who were beyond those walls.

Music has always been a strategy in war before the fighting army would deliver its death blow. Even our own U.S. Marines use music. The song "*Hell's Bells,*" by AC/DC, was blasted over loud speakers in Falluja before delivering the final strike to the Taliban in Baghdad. After ten years on the ground in Iraq following the war, the former New York Times journalist Dexter Filkin's writes in his book, "*The Forever War*":

> "*And then, as if from the depths, came a new sound: violent, menacing and dire. I looked back over my shoulder to where we had come from, into the vacant field at Falluja's northern edge. A group of marines were standing at the foot of a gigantic loudspeaker, the kind used at rock concerts. It was AC/DC, the Australian heavy metal band, pouring out its unbridled sounds. I recognized the song immediately: 'Hell Bells,' the band's celebration of satanic power, had come to us on the battlefield. Behind the strains of its guitars, a church bell tolled thirteen times.*"[19]

I refer to this writing to help us understanding that the Children of Israel, in my opinion, more than likely were not playing Christmas songs when they went to strike fear into the hearts of their enemies. They were more than likely playing music that let their enemies know that they are getting ready to die. Music, in war, has always been a strategy to strike fear in the hearts of the opponent. To make my point, here are a few lyrics in the song, "*Hell's Bells*" our Marines blasted before our enemies on loud concert speakers before they went after them:

> *I am a rolling thunder, a pouring rain*
> *I am comin' on like a hurricane*
> *My lightning's flashing across the sky*
> *You're only young but you're gonna die.*
>
> *I won't take no prisoners, won't spare no lives*
> *Nobody's putting up a fight*
> *I got my bell, I am gonna take you to hell*
> *I am gonna get ya, Satan get ya!*

How would you like to hear those words before a military campaign shows up at your door? Again, this was a strategy to

---

19   *The Forever War, page 3, Dexter Filkins*

accomplish their objective. I can imagine that it would strike to the very core of a man's heart knowing the fire and hell is getting ready to come. This is what the Children of Israel were coached to do by Joshua. Put the fear of God into your enemy's heart for several days and then go after them. We see high schools, colleges, and professional sports teams using music to motivate themselves against their opponent. This was a very good strategy and it worked. Good coaches always have great strategy.

The second strategy that Israel was given was to set an ambush behind their enemies at Ai. There would be a group of fighters who would approach the city and when the men of Ai would come out, the Israelites would flee from them. After they would flee, the Israelites who were in ambush behind the city would rise up and take the city while the men of Ai chased the first group of Israelites. They were directed to set it on fire, leaving the men of Ai nothing to return back home to. You can find all types of strategies the Lord gave Israel throughout the Bible when in times of war. The Lord, who is our greatest coach, has a strategy or blueprint for each one of us to win. We may have to lose sometimes on the path to becoming winners. The Lord never wastes any opportunity to teach His children to win in the name of Christ. We are more than conquerors. We are overcomers and victors in Him if we do not give up on living for Him.

CHAPTER 10

A Coach to Teach You Not to Watch the Opposition

"Let us fix our eyes on Jesus, the author and finisher of our faith."

~Hebrews 12:2

The things that I am about to share with you in this chapter can change your life. Even as I write, I am excited in anticipation about all the Lord is going to pour out to you concerning the subject of *"Not Paying Attention to Your Opponent."* I have coached for many years and have dealt with all types of people. There are principles in coaching sports that work in all areas of life. Watching where you keep your focus in order to accomplish your goal is very important. We all have our purpose and desires, but something I have noticed about many of us, whether we are in ministry, church, business, parenting, or athletics, is that we are distracted with watching the opposition instead of spending time focusing on what needs to be accomplished. I will not forget in 2007 when I was the Wide Receivers' coach for the Denver Titans, Colorado Football Conference Champions. That year, we were scheduled to play our most fierce opponent, the *Mile-High Grizzlies,* in a regular season game. We had edged them out the year before for the conference semi-finals game and went on to win the overall Championship for the State of Colorado. I taught a wide receiver corps philosophy; and with my receivers, we had gotten the attention of other teams in the league. It is a philosophy utilizing anywhere from six to nine receivers per game. The traditional way of coaching would use two to four receivers in a football game. I noticed that the Grizzlies' corner backs spent more time during the warm ups watching my receiving corps run routes, catch balls, and run plays prior to the kickoff than they spent getting ready for the game themselves. I realized we had their attention more than their own team and coaches. This is a common mistake most individuals make when they are concerned about their opponent. I immediately realized this was a crucial conference regular season game; but more importantly, I knew we would play them again for the conference championship. This team won that night as they successfully beat us 9-7. As disappointing as it was, I did not worry about it too much. There would be another day when we would play them when it really counted for advancement to championship night.

As I anticipated, on conference championship night came, I noticed that not only did the Grizzlies team watch our players take the field, warm up, and prepare, they also elected to take their time getting dressed and ready for the game themselves. They spent a lot of time watching us, thinking they had the game wrapped up, since they had beaten us already that year. They made the mistake of not paying attention to what they needed to do for preparation. One of my receivers walked over to me and said, "Coach, they are spending too much time watching what we are doing." I said to him, "It's okay; let us keep giving them something to watch." This would cost them dearly. We defeated them that night advancing ourselves once again to the State Championship game. Why is this so important? Too often I find people watching what others are doing instead of paying attention to what they should be doing themselves. It's one thing to watch your opponent to figure out what they are doing so you can defend yourself against them, it's another thing to watch them and forget about your own objectives, responsibilities and goals.

Also, we can learn a lesson of the importance of not paying attention to your opposition from the prophet Nehemiah. He had returned to Jerusalem to re-build the wall that had been burned down that protected his people, the Israelites. When he began his project, the bible says there was great opposition from Sanballat, Tobiah and Gesham. Regardless of many threats and mocking from his enemies, he succeeded in restoring the protection of Israel by leading a program to repair the holes in the wall. Despite their constant threats and requesting him to come down from working on the wall, he ignored their rhetoric and kept at his task. This is how we need to live our lives. When you have a purpose, we need to spend more time focusing on the task at hand not look at what others are saying and doing. When we pay attention to others we are no longer participators, but spectators. Spectators pay a price to watch a game. When we watch our competitors too long we too pay a price for watching them. A loss of time and a mind full of distractions. We must focus on what we are doing.

Coaches in our lives can make us aware of when we are distracted and not participating in this precious gift that God has given us. It's very easy to know when you are a spectator and not a participator. Some of the good tales tell signs if you are watching others are that spectators become critical and cynical. If you are finding yourself being very critical or cynical of a person that is because you are spending too much time watching them and not what you are assigned to do. This happens all too often. Know that your enemy is someone who has taken the liberty of being very critical of you. It's a free country, let them say what they want to say, as long as it is not true. It is even more dangerous when we do not know that we have an enemy. As long as you know who your enemies are, you can keep your eye on them. When we do not look at the person who is critical and cynical of us in this way, it can cause you a lot of life-long problems. Many times it will surprise you who has become your enemy. Regardless of who they are, never focus on what they are doing. Be mindful of them and keep an eye on them, but keep your focus on what you are doing to accomplish your life goals.

Jesus himself had many critics and cynics. He came tothe world to die for the sins of the world. He did not have time to pay attention to the Pharisees, Sadducees, and the Jews who hated and wanted to kill him. The success of his assignment came through his ability to focus on his Father's will. People, businesses, ministries, marriages or teams who pay attention to others lose sight of their own purpose. Success will elude them and defeat is inevitable. Life is a game of wins and losses. In each one, you can choose to not pay attention to the opposition.

The writer in the book of Hebrews tells the saints to focus their eyes on Jesus, who is the author and finisher of their faith.[20] This is true even for our spiritual success and development. I cannot tell you how

20   Hebrews 12:2

many times I was tempted to waste time watching the unbelievable, satanic attacks of those who proclaimed to be sons and daughters of God. All I can say is that if you're not careful, you will be struck with amazement at times and find yourself in a spectator role. Never watch the opposition, always stay focused on your purpose.

Life is not as long as we think. Focusing on what you are here to do is paramount. Learn to love people, but not so much that you lose sight of your purpose. Teams and individuals who win concentrate on where they are trying to go. They know and keep their objectives in perspective. At a church service revival held at my church several years ago, Evangelist Tim Storey said something I never forgot: *"Where you point your satellite dish, that's what you pick up."*[21] If you think about those who use a satellite dish on their roof to pick up television stations, it will not work unless it is pointed in the right direction. If our hearts and minds are not pointed in the direction they should be, we too will not pick up on the signal the Father is trying to get over to us. Maybe this explains why so many ask me from time to time why they cannot hear God like others do? It may be that their heart, thoughts and minds are pointed in the wrong direction. You can pick up on the wrong signals. Cease from watching those who compete against and trouble you. Make a commitment to focus on the plans God has for you and not watch the opposition.

---

21   *Evangelist Tim Storey*

CHAPTER 11

A Coach to Teach You How to Stay Calm

"The quiet words of the wise are more to be heeded than the shouts of a leader of fools."

~Ecclesiastes 9:17

The world is going through one of its most challenging times economically. The need for economic recovery is not only a national concern, but has become a global concern as well. Every nation under the sun has suffered from the economic struggles, including third-world countries who depend so much on export business that create jobs. The increased unemployment and revelation of corrupt CEOs and bankers have only added fuel to the already heated fire. The world is starting to witness countless acts of violence due to the anger and frustration of economic loss. Outside of these issues, men and women are clearly expressing themselves out of their anxious souls. While coaching boys and men in the very physical game of football, I recognized an element of the game that separated the winners from the losers. My many years of coaching and observation has always lead me back to this distinct fact: "The teams who learned how to remain calm in the midst of chaos or a bad game had more opportunity to think through, correct their mistakes, and ultimately turn the game around. It is not what you do when things are going well, it is how you respond when trouble comes."We are living in a much less coached society. Do not lose yourself during the tough economic times you may be experiencing today. When stress and anxiety come, there is a greater need for leaders who remain calm in the midst of crisis. Staying calm is not a gift, it is a learned behavior developed after considering the results of many experiences in your life. Unfortunately, it is one of the most difficult characteristics to get others to understand its value. In our capitalistic society, 80 percent of the jobs in America are in the customer service realm. What happened to the American dream? The problem is that only few are experiencing it. The medium income in America is $51,000/yr. People who are experiencing the American dream are making close to $130,000 per year or more. This means that if you are making less than $51,000 a year, you are not close to the dream that we were told in school we can have if we worked hard. If most of us are working in customer service related positions, it is going to be rather difficult to increase our incomes above $130,000/ year. This could be the reason why so many are stressing out about their financial future in America.For many years, I have understood that man is mostly guided by his emotions. Our emotions are very complex and oftentimes work against us instead of for us. People who believe in what they feel create many problems for not only themselves, but for those who are closely connected to them. On the contrary, I have watched those who have emotions, but do not let them overtake who they really are, accomplish their objectives more often than most. Know this, nothing good is ever born out of emotional chaos and confusion. To value calmness and teach people to be calm will be a noble task only if we can get it into the hearts and souls of the masses. This is a much needed characteristic not only for the intellectual or the elite, but for every breathing and living person on the face of their earth. In truth, many do not handle things well when difficulty shows up in our lives. Learning to diffuse unbridled emotions in a man is a much needed art in today's society. This is where good coaching comes in. In my experience, the art of coaching is not just learning "how to" strategies to win a game. It has more to do with knowing how to coach your players through adversity. A calm, cool headed and collected coach is able to do more with a group of men and women than meets the eye. Winning can have more to do with self-control than with mere talent. I have witnessed that talent alone does not guarantee success. I have been around men who had a lot of talent, but could not fight themselves out of a paper bag because they had no self control. Their emotions ruled them; and therefore, would always get the best of them at the most critical times. Likewise, I have experienced less talented players who you can teach self-control. They win games that if you looked at the line ups on paper, they should not have. If you look at today's National Football League and National Basketball Association, the teams that have the calmest head coaches seem to be winning the Super Bowls and NBA Finals. The point I am trying to make is that if you look at coaching and leadership qualities of winning coaches, you would have to agree that they have an undeniable ability to keep themselves and the others around them centered, calm, and focused. Not everyone has this kind of gift. This is a God given gift. The Apostle James tells us:

> *"Every good and perfect gift is from above, coming down from the Father of the heavenly lights, who does not change like shifting shadows."*

Notice the Apostle is talking about more than one gift. We need coaches that can lead. More importantly, we need the kind of coaches in our lives who can keep their heads in the midst of trouble. These are troubling times for most around the world. I pray that our leaders do not lose control. Coaches who can see the light at the end of the tunnel keep their composure. It does not mean that they are always right; it just means that they can see something that others around them cannot. It is these kinds of eyes that lead people to success and victory. Giving up, throwing in the towel, and seeing everything as "doom and gloom" never helps anyone. When you have a calm coach in your life, it means that you have someone who has "vision." In fact, the Word teaches us:

"Where there is no revelation, the people cast off restraint; but blessed is he who keeps the law.[22] The word revelation in this verse means "vision." A person who has no vision loses self-control. They cast off restraint; they see everything as a hopeless matter. The reason that they see things this way is because they are not able to keep themselves. Happy is the man who can keep himself or herself. Keeping ourselves has everything to do with keeping your emotions. How unfortunate it is today to see so many losing their mind, emotions, and will over such trivial matters. The economic crisis we are experiencing has people committing suicide and horrible acts of violence. I thank God for heady coaches in my life; men and women with whom I can sit and have a

---

stress free conversation that leads to a clear path of direction. Life is not always easy. Know that things will come into your life to disrupt your calm. You must understand it, recognize it, and resist losing yourself in the midst of the chaos.

CHAPTER 12

A Coach's Experience is Better than Your Ignorance

"My people are destroyed from lack of knowledge. Because you have rejected knowledge, I also reject you as my priests; because you have ignored the law of your God, I also will ignore your children."

~Hosea 4:6

The story of the prophet Hosea has always been an interesting piece of history to me regarding God's relationship with a prophet; in particular, the extreme requests God would ask to show the prophet what His relationship was like with the nation of Israel. Many times in the Bible God refers to Israel as a wife or a bride. In the book of Hosea, God tells the prophet, *"Go, take to yourself an adulterous wife and children of unfaithfulness, because the land is guilty of the vilest adultery in departing from the Lord."*[23]

What a bizarre command it seemed for God to give to one of His holy prophets. For many years it confused me why God would ask the man of God to do this such a thing. Not only did God tell Hosea to marry a whore, but to make children of unfaithfulness. As if an adulterous wife was not bad enough, He wanted him to have unfaithful children. Let us look at the essence of why God asked the prophet to do this.

If you read the book of Hosea in its entirety, you will see the prophet has a very difficult marriage with his wife Gomer who was a prostitute. Gomer loves the excitement and lure of financial gain in prostitution. She also loves the safety and security of being married to her husband— Hosea. In her duplicity, she goes back and forth

---

23   *(Hosea 1:2).*

between the two lives. Each time, God sent Hosea out in the streets to find his wife, clean her up, and take her back. Gomer, at times, comes to her senses when things get too bad on the streets and reasoned to herself that it would be better to go back home to her husband. It was a crazy cycle, but Hosea was instructed by the Lord to love and forgive his wife each time. It took me years to realize the point God wanted to get over to his prophet. Until we begin to experience what God feels, we will never know and understand the Lord. We think we know God, but it is not until you have to love and forgive people who betray you, are constantly unfaithful to you, and who use you at their leisure, will you begin to know the Lord. It is in our taking upon His yoke that we begin to learn of him.

To God, we are all like the wife Gomer and the unfaithful children. God is represented in the prophet Hosea. God wanted the prophet to know firsthand the hurt and pain He experiences when his wife (the children of Israel) and children are back and forth, serving other gods, and are not committed to Him. It would have been one thing for God to teach the prophet this, but it was another for Hosea to experience this for himself. God knew the experience from this feat would register better with Hosea than words could ever say. To be honest with you, until we all experience certain things, we really do not understand it very much at all. God wanted the prophet to know what it was like to extend his arm to a wife and children in whom he loved so much, only for each time to see them turn away and go after other gods. This was a very painful experience for the prophet. How could this happen when he would love his wife and children so much? Why would they not want to stay at home in the safety and security of the Lord? Unfortunately, this was a lesson that God wanted him to understand. Only experience would do this time around.

God saw the violation of Israel as real as an adulterous wife who constantly breaches covenant with her husband and unruly unfaithful children to their father. God knew these two examples would create a clear picture of how God sees His people. There can be nothing more painful to a husband than to experience a wife whose love is for others and is consistently double-minded about whether to leave or stay with her husband. Likewise, a faithful father who raises children who are unfaithful to him can be equally as tormenting. In these two descriptions lie the true emotional experience God was dealing with man. Until the prophet Hosea had become familiar with the same, he would have no real understanding on how important it would be for him to turn Israel back to God. Much of Israel's trouble stemmed from their duplicity and ignorance.

I use the word ignorance with extreme care, because I understand how many people view the word and its meaning. For hundreds and hundreds of years in this country, the last thing you wanted to be considered was *"ignorant."* The word carries so much taboo that many kids today will not ask questions in a classroom setting when they realize they do not know something. I want to shed revelation on what ignorance truly is; and although dangerous, how it can be overcome. If you look at the word and break it apart, we see it has one main part *"ignore."* To ignore something means to *not pay attention to, to not regard, to go unnoticed,* to reject.[24] When I received the true revelation of this word, I realized every man has the power to be knowledgeable or ignorant of whatever he or she chooses.

I realized that ignorance has very little to do with brain power and has more to do with what we did not or refuse to pay attention to. Let me say it like this. There will be many that read this book who I will never know because there is no way that I can know everyone that comes across this book. That means that I would be ignorant of each person reading this book that I do not know. However, if I meet some of you and spend time with you, I would have the power or option to get to know you. If I choose to get to know you this means that I have made it a point to pay attention to you. If we pay attention to something or anyone long enough, good or bad, there is no way that you will continue to be ignorant of them. This is exactly what Israel was doing in the prophet Hosea's day. They had become ignorant of God because they choose to ignore Him and His word. Their ignorance was because they did not want to pay attention to God.

Israel was constantly coached by God's servants throughout history to pay attention to His word. Let us look at a few reminders from Moses:

---

24   *Merriam-Webster Online*

> *"These are the commands, decrees and laws the Lord your God directed me to teach you to observe in the land that you are crossing the Jordan to possess, so that you, your children and their children after them may fear the Lord your God as long as you live by keeping all his decrees and commands that I give you, and so that you may enjoy long life. Hear, O Israel, and be careful to obey so that it may go well with you and that you may increase greatly in a land flowing with milk and honey, just as the Lord, the God of your fathers, promised you."* [25]

> *"Be careful to follow every command I am giving you today, so that you may live and increase and may enter and possess the land that the Lord promised on oath to your forefathers."* [26]

> *"Observe the commands of the Lord your God, walking in his ways and revering him."* [27]

Joshua, the servant of the Lord, was reminded of the same by the Lord:

> *"Be careful to obey all the law my servant Moses gave you; do not turn from it to the right or to the left, that you may be successful wherever you go. Do not let this Book of the Law depart from your mouth; meditate on it day and night, so that you may be careful to do everything written in it."* [28]

These are just a few examples of what has been said about paying attention to God's word throughout Israel's history. Regardless of the many warnings they received from all of the Major and Minor Prophets, in Hosea's time, the violation was again "*the lack of knowledge*" of God's word. He gives us a clue why they lacked the knowledge of the word. It did not have anything to do with being born with downs syndrome, attention deficit syndrome, schizophrenia, bipolar-syndrome, mental disturbance, o being motherless or fatherless. It had everything to do

---

25   *Deuteronomy 6:1-3*
26   *Deuteronomy 6:1-3*
27   *Deuteronomy 8:6*
28   *Joshua 1:7.*

with them *"ignoring"* God's word. They refused to pay attention to it. In fact, the Lord said to them in so few words:

> *"Since you ignored me and rejected my word, I am going to not only ignore you and reject you, but I am also going to ignore and reject your children."* [29]

I said all of the above to paint a picture. A coach brings us experience from the things they have learned to pay attention to that our ignorance or inexperience cannot afford to continue in. I would much rather pay attention and listen to the experience of someone who has done what I am trying to accomplish, than to be stuck in my own lack of knowledge. There is so much experience around us each and every-day. Many of you reading this book know what it is like to sit in the barbershop or beauty salon and listen to older people who have experience. We know what it's like to sit in classrooms, courtrooms, family reunions, churches, and counselor offices and glean from those with the experience. Unfortunately, this generation has very little desire to listen to those with the experience; therefore, it is leaving them ignorant. Coaches are the ones in our lives with the experience. Their experiences can have monumental results in our lives if we only listen to their concerned voices. I never wasted or tossed away the experience of an older person. It has helped me get through so many things in my own life. We have a choice to choose the ignorance within ourselves or the experience of others that God places in our lives. I have found that the experience has a greater value than the ignorance.

In my opinion, everybody does need a coach. We need them to guide us through the different trials and tribulations we will have in life. Gleaning from a coach's knowledge can make the journey much smoother. I will end this book with a timely testimony I received from a young man by the name of Justin. I coached Justin for one year in semi-professional football. Justin had played as a wide receiver for a few years in the Colorado Football Conference league and was virtually a no-name player throughout the state. I was transferred to his team as a wide receiver coach due to the previous owners I had coached with for two years partnering with the ownership for the team Justin was on— The Denver Pirates. I had approximately twenty-five young men try out for wide receiver that year in training camp. I knew a

29   *Hosea 4:6*

few of them, but like Justin, many I did not know. As tryout season dwindled down and cuts were made, I noticed that Justin was still in the running to become one of the nine players I would choose for my receiver corps. Justin worked really hard in camp to make the roster and I noticed that he would listen when I spoke. In my mind, he still needed a lot of work to move up the depth chart. He would at the time be my eighth or ninth man in the rotation. This team had a lot of veterans and guys that could play. I kept working with all the receivers and noticed that Justin was paying extra attention to when I would demonstrate how the receivers were to run each pass route. In a semi-professional league, you get players from different experiences and backgrounds. Unfortunately, many have been trained incorrectly, or have never been trained at all, and have some bad habits that are hard to break. How fast Justin was catching on to what I would demonstrate caught my attention, so he began to move up on the depth chart. He moved to sixth on the chart in a matter of a few weeks. We had a pre-season game coming up soon and I wanted to know who would be my top four receivers. Two more weeks passed and Justin now moved up to the fourth receiver. We traveled to Albuquerque, New Mexico to play our only pre-season game. His performance that night, with three touchdowns, was unbelievable. This performance would move him to being my number one or two receiver; to get ready for our season opener. To make this testimony short, our team went undefeated that year, 10-0. Not including what our running backs and defense put on the board each game, our receiver corps averaged 28 points a game. As a team, we averaged 45 points per game. Justin went on to lead the Colorado Football Conference in receptions, yards per catch and touch downs per game. He accomplished two to three touchdown catches per game. Some games he had four touchdowns catches. He was the top receiver that year in the semi-professional league for the state of Colorado. I asked Justin to explain to a friend of mine how he went from a no-name receiver to the most respected and feared that year? Justin told my friend that when I came in as the receiver coach, I changed everything. He said he saw early on that all he had to do was "listen" to what I was saying to them as their coach and it would work not only for him, but for the rest of the wide receivers corps. I share this testimony from Justin because it came to me in a timely manner as I was finishing this book. Coincidentally, Justin recently became a father and moved into a lower level unit of the condominium complex I have been living in for the past four years. He told my friend and I that he has not had another year like that as a wide receiver since the year (2005) I coached him. We advanced to the Colorado Football Conference championship that year playing the Denver Titans who had not lost a championship game in six years. The first play from scrimmage, we threw a 55 yard strike down the middle of the field to Justin that he ran for the touchdown. This shocked the entire stadium on championship night. We ended up in a dog fight for the rest of the game against the Titans falling short of the win, 19-15. Nevertheless, this undefeated regular season, as well as the amount of points my receiver corps delivered per game, set the tone for the next two years. The ownership I coached for purchased the Denver Titans. We came into the league with maybe four original Titans; the rest were new players. We won the Colorado Football Conference Championship for the next two years with new players. I went on to coach a few more average receivers who became exceptional and most valuable players in the state and made the All-Star team. One in particular, named Troy, who accomplished this honor twice with me as his coach. I share these stories because they are very fitting to what this book is all about. Both, Justin and Troy were avid listeners and accomplished things in football which took them from the place of average to the most feared and respected players on the field in the state, in a league that was full of talent.

In closing, it does not matter how old we get or what experience we have, the important thing to know is "Everybody Needs a Coach."

ABOUT THE AUTHOR

Kenneth Bordeaux was born in Buffalo, New York in August of 1963, to Arthur C. Williams and Carol F. Bordeaux. He was raised by his mother and Uncle Dennis C. Bordeaux in Rochester, New York until he graduated High School and enlisted in the United States Air Force.

He honorably served under the Ronald Reagan Administration for seven years. Kenneth knew he was a long way from the housing projects in upstate New York, when on December 7, 1987, he found himself standing on the White House front lawn, as the Flight Officer in charge, for the United States Air Force Honor Guard. He stood a mere thirty yards away from President Reagan and Russia's President, Mikhal Gorbachev. The two were historically meeting in America for the first time to open the Washington Summit. This summit would be the time when Reagan and Gorbachev would sign the INF treaty, which eliminated 4% of both Superpowers' nuclear arsenals. It was the first U.S.—Soviet treaty to provide for destruction of nuclear weapons, for on-site monitoring of the destruction. This would be one of those moments in his life when he had to ask God, "Lord, what are you trying to show me? What in the world am I doing here?"

After President Reagan's second term, Kenneth felt very strongly about not serving under another President while in the armed forces. He knew he had just miraculously served under the administration of one of the greatest Presidents to ever live, so he decided to cherish the experience, and was discharged from the Air Force in April, 1988.

A year later, he moved from the Washington DC/ Maryland area to Denver, Colorado. It would be there, years later, that he would launch and pastorthe Unity House of Prayer Christian Center—a.k.a. "A Church With-out Walls" for the next ten years. He has a strong passion and desire to teach God's people the principles and disciplines of the Word of God. Kenneth was not raised in the Church, but became a Christian at age twenty, while in the military. He saw that many Christians who did grow up in church did not value the principles and teachings that had been made available to them for so many years.

He was astonished when he read in Jeremiah 8:11, regarding the priest and the prophet,

"They treat the wound of my people as though it was not serious."

Kenneth realized this as being the same problem in today's church. The people are not serious. The pastors are not serious. Very few are serious. He desired to bring a positive change to the teaching and obedience of God's Word that has been missing in the Church. Through the years, he became very active in neighborhood outreach, evangelism, and community support. None of these came easy for him. All came at a tremendous price.

Kenneth also has a great love and passion for the sport of football. He played Pop Warner as a skinny child and became the Defensive Captain during his senior year, at Jefferson High School in Rochester, New York. He has invested eighteen years in coaching and developing players in the sport. He spent twelve years coaching youth ages 5-14 and another five years coaching adult men in the Colorado Football Minor League Conference where he wasa wide receivers coach and has won two CFC Championships in 2006 and 2007. He uses the platform of sports and coaching to minister to young men and spread the love of Christ.

KENNETH G. BORDEAUX